What Every Library Director Should Know

Susan Carol Curzon

ROWMAN & LITTLEFIELD
Lanham • Boulder • New York • Toronto • Plymouth, UK

Published by Rowman & Littlefield
4501 Forbes Boulevard, Suite 200, Lanham, Maryland 20706
www.rowman.com

10 Thornbury Road, Plymouth PL6 7PP, United Kingdom

Copyright © 2014 by Rowman & Littlefield

British Library Cataloguing in Publication Information Available

Library of Congress Cataloging-in-Publication Data

Curzon, Susan Carol.
What every library director should know / Susan Carol Curzon.
pages cm
Includes index.
ISBN 978-0-8108-9310-8 (cloth : alk. paper) – ISBN 978-0-8108-9187-6 (pbk. : alk. paper) – ISBN
978-0-8108-9188-3 (ebook)
1. Library administration. I. Title.
Z678.C888 2014
025.1–dc23
2013047163

∞™ The paper used in this publication meets the minimum requirements of American
National Standard for Information Sciences Permanence of Paper for Printed Library
Materials, ANSI/NISO Z39.48-1992.

Printed in the United States of America

This book is dedicated with love to
Sophia Noor Dillabaugh and
Braeden Alexander Dillabaugh

Contents

Acknowledgments

I want to thank my husband, Dr. M. B. Taher Ayati, for reviewing many drafts of this book and for providing me with important suggestions and changes. I also thank him, as always, for his support for all of my projects and goals.

I would like to express my thanks to my long time friend and colleague, Dr. Kathleen Dunn, who read the first draft of this book and provided very valuable insight and advice. I also wish to thank my brother, Peter J. Curzon, Chief of Police in Astoria, for providing expert knowledge related to police and emergency matters.

Thanks as always to Charles Harmon, executive editor for Rowman & Littlefield, for his continued encouragement. Charles has been the editor for each one of my books and I have always appreciated his knowledge and experience. My thanks as well to Lara Graham, assistant editor at R&L, Ayleen Stellhorn, and Sylvia Cannizzaro for their work on this book.

I appreciate so much the many excellent colleagues with whom I worked throughout my career especially in the County of Los Angeles Public Library; the City of Glendale (CA) Public Library; the California State University, Northridge, Oviatt Library; and the California State University system. Their continued dedication and commitment made work a pleasure. I now have the privilege of enjoying their friendship in retirement.

QUOTE ATTRIBUTIONS

I want to thank the following library directors, deans, administrators, and faculty who graciously provided quotes in response to my question "What is the one piece of management wisdom that you would give to anyone who wishes to become, or who is, a library director?" Their quotes are dispersed throughout the book and provide true pearls of wisdom that every library director should know.

Dr. Camila A. Alire
    Dean Emerita, University of New Mexico
    ALA President, 2009–2010
Steve Brogden
    Director
    Thousand Oaks Library
    Thousand Oaks, CA
Jon E. Cawthorne, Ph.D.
    Associate Dean for Public Service and Assessment
    Florida State University Libraries
Connie Vinita Dowell
    Dean of Libraries
    Vanderbilt University
G. Edward Evans
    University Librarian (Retired)
    Loyola Marymount University
Rod Hersberger
    Library Dean Emeritus
    California State University, Bakersfield
    ALA Treasurer 2007–2010

Marsha Gelman Kmec, B.S., M.L.I.S.
  Director of Library Services (1992–2012)
  Olive View/UCLA Medical Center
  Health Sciences Library
Peter Hepburn
  Head Librarian
  College of the Canyons
  Santa Clarita, CA
Luis Herrera
  City Librarian
  San Francisco Public Library
Penny S. Markey, M.S.L.S.
  Library Administrator, Youth Services, Cultural Programming
  & Productivity (Retired)
  County of Los Angeles Public Library
Elizabeth Martinez
  Library and Community Services Director
  Salinas, CA
  Former Executive Director of the American Library Association
Sue McKnight, Ph.D.
  Director
  Sue McKnight Consulting
  Melbourne, Australia
Eleanor Mitchell
  Director of Library Services
  Dickinson College
  Carlisle, PA
James L. Mullins
  Dean of Libraries and Esther Ellis Norton Professor
  Purdue University
Laurel Patric
  Director of Libraries (Retired)
  Glendale (CA) Public Library

Brian E. C. Schottlaender
  The Audrey Geisel University Librarian
  University of California, San Diego
Margaret Donnellan Todd
  County Librarian
  County of Los Angeles Public Library
Phil Turner, Ed.D.
  Professor Emeritus
  University of North Texas
  College of Information
Scott Walter, M.L.S., Ph.D.
  University Librarian
  DePaul University
  Editor-in-Chief, *College and Research Libraries*
Virginia A. Walter, Ph.D.
  Professor Emerita
  University of California, Los Angeles
  Information Studies Department
Sandra G. Yee
  Dean, Wayne State University Libraries and Wayne State
  University School of Library and Information Science

Introduction

What Every Library Director Should Know

Most LIS graduate programs offer a course in the management of a library. In such courses, we learn important management concepts and practices in budgeting, supervising, marketing, customer services, decision making, and other necessary functions. Such courses are critical in giving beginning librarians grounding in the study of management. After all, many librarians will go on in their career to various kinds of supervision and management work. These starter courses introduce us to the complex study of management thought, theory, and practice.

However, anyone who has ever held any kind of management position, such as managing a program, directing a grant, or running the entire library, can tell you that understanding the basics of management is not enough to be successful on the job. Not only do we need to continue our study of management, but we also need to understand the unwritten rules, the unwritten strategies, and the unwritten wisdom which are gained on the job, learned by observing others, or, if the librarian is very fortunate, taught by a mentor. Sometimes this knowledge, finally gained, comes at too high a price or is learned too late. A career inexplicably stalled, a desired position not gained, the failure to thrive in a current position can leave us puzzled, confused, and hurt. After all, we worked hard every day. Every day, we concentrated on the job, often sacrificing time with family and friends. What went wrong?

These are the issues answered in this book. This is not a conventional management text. You will not get, for example, the history of management, the basics of budgeting, or personnel and labor laws. Instead my focus is on nuances of behavior, political strategies, common wisdom, mentor-like advice, and the subtle codes, which, when paired with other management skills, will bring increased chances of success on the job and throughout your career.

It does not matter what type of library you are in—management is management, wisdom is wisdom. *What Every Library Director Should Know* is the insider's view of vital actions, behaviors, and strategies to succeed in every type of library. The content is based extensively on my direct experience after a long career in several types of libraries but also on my observation of experiences that happened to others. Additionally, fellow directors, colleagues, faculty, bosses, library supporters and customers, and board members have been generous across the years in sharing with me some of their best, worst, and most meaningful of experiences.

If you have picked up this book, chances are you already are a library director seeking additional understanding or confirmation of your actions or you are a librarian who has a vision of yourself as a director. In either case, you want to make a positive difference and you want both your career and your library to flourish. This book will help to get you there by explaining and illustrating the wisdom that is mostly unwritten and that mostly moves in subtle communication.

You have worked hard to get where you are, and I hope that this book will help you to go the rest of the way.

Chapter One

At the Helm

Well, here you are—or soon will be—at the helm of the library. It will now be your responsibility to deliver library service to thousands of customers. Generally speaking, most library operations run well because libraries are filled with competent and dedicated staff with a genuine wish to help the customers. But no one would interpret this as a license to sit back and watch the world go by. Enduring quality library service requires significant vigilance. Policies must still be developed, staff trained, resources deployed, collections developed, and customers heard—in short, core functions of every kind must continually occur with good management.

In addition, what every library director should know is that close attention must be paid to a handful of strategies that will secure the quality of service and thereby success at the helm. These strategies are rarely in the library management texts, but if we miss these strategies, we might be caught by surprise as the service we once thought was so good takes a downward turn.

UNBUCKLE THE ORGANIZATION

Most libraries exist within a much larger parent organization, and many of these parent organizations are substantial bureaucracies.

What is a bureaucracy? It is an organization that is characterized by a clear hierarchy, written and sometimes inflexible rules and regulations, and often a well-defined division of labor. Once established, bureaucracies are often resistant to change. Bureaucracies also have two other defining characteristics—they have an endless inclination to increase and an endless inclination to centralize power. The natural consequence is larger and larger bureaucracies.

However, the irony is that while libraries are surrounded by bureaucracies, they are often bureaucracies also. Just as our parent organizations increase their rules and regulations and centralize power, libraries do so too. And therein lays the danger. What every library director should know is how carefully we have to watch the bureaucracy increasing within our own libraries. Why? What is the problem with increasing bureaucracy?

An increasingly hardening bureaucracy is symptomatic of a declining life cycle. All organizations have a life cycle. They are born, grow, mature, and wither. Sometimes the life cycle is long and sometimes short. How many community programs or businesses have you seen that once were successful yet end with a whimper? How many corporations that were once global powerhouses have seen themselves overtaken by an upstart?

Right now, you might be getting kudos on the quality of your library. Ironically, just when everything is going well is just when we are at the most vulnerable. Libraries at their height of ability and prestige are at risk because they are simultaneously aging. New trends, strategies, and technology are surging forward always. Always, there are new competitors on the market. Always the expectations of customers are changing. Ask yourself, "Where am I in this cycle?"

In order to answer this, think whether you can still answer yes to these questions: Is your library able to respond rapidly to changes? Do good new ideas move quickly from concept to approval? Are customers impressed with the speed of resolution of their issues? Is the staff satisfied that their ideas are being heard? Are policies flexible? Does staff have the capability to bend policy when needed? Are decisions always made to improve customer service versus being made for the convenience of the staff? Are users only a few clicks away from getting what they want versus mind-boggling multiple clicks? Does the staff feel that they are involved in decision making? Do staff and customers feel that they know what is going on in the library?

If you answered no to any of these, then you might already be pedaling toward the downward cycle. If you keep going on that trajectory, the library will lose its current relevance and will grow stale. Once that happens, other forces begin to gather. Apart from the obvious restlessness of the staff and the customers, bosses begin to pick up on what is happening and they begin to think. They begin to think about merging the library with another department. They begin to make plans for reallocating library space. They begin to look at closures of branches or departments. Yes, many times these are fiscally driven ideas, but behind that is their clear thought that the library is not as relevant and certainly not as powerful as it once was.

So, it is time to take action and that action is to unbuckle the organization.

What does it mean to unbuckle the organization? What it really means is that your library increases its responsiveness to the constantly changing internal and external environment. It has flexibility and can travel quickly in its responses. In other words, it stays up with what is happening. The bottom line to unbuckling is to guarantee through a series of strategies the library's continued relevance. This way, the library is always refreshed—instead of going down the path toward the end of its life cycle, it is reinvigorated and replenished.

Let's look at these strategies to unbuckle the library.

You already know that you have to listen continually to what the customers want through regular cycles of assessment. You can never cease increasing your relevance to existing customers. However, you cannot stop there. You must also extend the body of people to whom you listen. Take these examples: When was the last time that you listened to people who are not customers of the library? They can tell you a lot about why they don't use the library. If you are in a library that serves kids, when was the last time that you listened to children? At a surprisingly young age, they can articulate what they need. Do take a leaf out of the book from businesses. The best businesses never cease looking for new customers.

Next, continually create a dynamic open environment in which ideas from many sources flow into your library. You already know the importance of scanning the wealth of information available from our professional associations, journals, and colleagues near and far as well as what the professionals in information technology are talking about. They have to be on the cutting edge to survive, so your continued awareness of their issues is very useful for spotting trends. Keep up with best practices in management too because you will gain many good ideas and strategies that will be helpful as a director. Be especially mindful of the trends and changing needs of your parent organization. Read those company reports, attend company events, and stay up with company news.

Sue McKnight: "Leadership requires a vision and goals. Without a direction, you can waste a great deal of time going nowhere! To help define that vision, ask library customers as well as staff, how they would define what an ideal library service looks like. The more involved people are with defining a vision, the more acceptance and buy-in you'll have with implementing changes required to achieve the vision. Make sure staff understand that they help create the future!"

Do remember that the business of gathering ideas is not something the director does alone. Encourage all of the staff to be engaged in awareness of new ideas—all eyes and ears have to be looking and listening as to what is going on in the various environments in which the library dwells. Let the staff introduce new ideas, new perspectives, and new solutions. Praise them for their ideas. Staff who feel that they are helping to create a vibrant and changing library are far more likely to be actively engaged and interested in the library's future.

In order to achieve staff participation, do find time and money for staff to attend conferences, workshops, or online training even when time and money are tight. Training is a soft target for budget reductions but it is a wrong corner to cut. Training is an investment not an expense. It is an investment in your library's continuing relevance. And don't be the director who goes to every conference when the staff have few funds for travel.

Another strategy is to be in a continual cycle of management review of the various services and functions of the library. I am not talking about a formal report, even though that may have its purposes. What I am talking about here is simulating the experience of the customers of that service. Sit down and pretend to be a customer. Go through the processes and experience what the customer experiences. Is the path to service delivery convoluted and long or clear and fast? If you understandably don't have the time to do this, get a trusted staff member to do so and report to you. If you are in a university setting, professors may be willing to have this as a class project.

While you are at it, ask these questions: What is the fill rate for the service? What is the response time? What is the level of satisfaction?

Of course, all of this is done openly with the staff with the clear understanding that this isn't about identifying failures and pointing fingers but instead about growing the service. When you have identified what is needed, then resources can begin to flow toward that need. Of course, you do have to follow up. Don't let this just be a passing exercise.

Don't forget about the behind-the-scenes services of the library such as acquisitions, cataloging, and processing. The customers might never see or know about these functions, but they feel their effect such as when resources take too long to be accessible. Study the work flow and reengineer any processes that are creating a lag or duplication. Remember that reengineering should not be a one-time project but instead a process of continuous improvement.

Keep in mind that your staff are also internal customers of each other's functions and services. In particular, be attentive to a staff disheartened by overly bureaucratic administrative processes. While the parent organization might be the source of stringent rules and regulations, it is important for every library director to take a look at the administrative processes of the library. What is the length of time for staff to be reimbursed for travel? What is the length of time for supplies to arrive? How long does it take for equipment to be repaired? Don't wait for the staff to complain but instead treat the staff as customers and find out what the issues are. Then correct those issues.

In order to unbuckle the library, the ideas must reach you. The next strategy then is to take a good hard look at how ideas and issues flow in your library. Are you the last to know? Do you sometimes hear staff say that they suggested that idea months ago? Or complained about something weeks ago? Were you surprised by a serious matter that you should have heard about? If so, then there is a problem. A conversation with fellow managers and staff would be called for here—a clear understanding of what the director needs communicated as well as the speed of that communication. Of course, you can't just make this point once and think that is it—this is a matter that requires regular attention.

While you are listening to their feedback, consider that it might also be something that you are doing that is blocking the flow of ideas. Be honest with yourself. Have you overbooked your calendar so much that staff can't get in to see you quickly? Are reports and ideas sitting around for so long without any response from you that they are no longer relevant? This is an idea killer for sure. After a while, people will begin to simply shrug their shoulders at attempts to improve the idea flow. Remember it is important not to stir up the organization with discussions on improving the idea flow when there is no intent of following through.

Let's note two concerns here. You might have a situation in which the middle managers are the weak link in communication. Training and continual emphasis of the importance of rapid communication may be called for because a hardened layer of middle managers is a real cork in the flow of ideas. Consider in the training the question of why the communication isn't flowing. Is it because the middle managers don't understand the importance of the information or ideas that you need? Are they holding onto information and ideas as a way of gathering power? More often than not, it is because they don't see the relevance of the information to your work because they may have only a very small idea of what the director's job really is.

Here is one temptation you want to avoid: when ideas are not flowing to you from the middle managers, it is sometimes tempting to go around them as roadblocks. However, jumping the line of authority and going directly to their staff, while it might work in the short run, is always problematic in the long run. When a director bypasses managers, the message is clear—they are not respected and that message will serve you very badly in the future. After all, if you don't respect the managers, the staff won't either. The result is that the staff will start to jump the line too and try to report to you directly, even if not overtly, which will disrupt the normal work flow process and tangle you in minutiae. Untangling what you now have started will be difficult, because staff always enjoy access to power and will not easily give even a little bit up. Additionally, the resentment of the middle managers toward you will grow, and they then may consciously begin to close you off from important communication, which, in turn, will create the roadblock that you tried to solve in the first place. Just remember that going around middle managers is just avoiding the problem and that problem will come back to bite you if you don't really solve it.

The second concern is that people also have to know that not every idea that is brought up will be implemented. Again, training and open discussion is important here. People have to know that all kinds of ideas must flow, must bounce against each other and then finally must be prioritized in terms of the goals and the resources. People do understand, but it is best to articulate this so that there is no misunderstanding about what happens when ideas or concerns are presented.

Importantly, remember that once you have addressed these concerns, it isn't over. As a director, there is no rest for you. Unbuckling the library and continually focusing on its relevance is a never-ending quest.

THE IMPORTANCE OF MAKING A GOOD IMPRESSION

All our lives, we are aware of the importance of making a good impression. However superficial it might seem, we are judged by others continually as a result of the impression that we are making. If we make a good impression, we are respected and admired. If we make a bad impression, we are discounted and disregarded.

The same is true of library services. Customers can quickly and easily form either good or bad impressions of our services. If we want our libraries to be well respected, to be points of pride, to be held in esteem, and to be appreciated and valued, then we must be in the business of making a good impression.

Making a good impression has two dimensions: the first impression and the lasting impression. A good first impression naturally influences the lasting impression that the customers have.

Let's talk about making a good first impression. Certainly, we all know the importance of making a good first impression. We dress up for interviews, we look good for first dates, we are on our best behavior the first time we meet potential in-laws. There is a good reason for it—a negative impression, especially at the beginning, is hard to overcome.

Now, you might be saying to yourself, "I am comfortable that we are delivering good service with a strong collection and good staff. What more is needed?" This is where acute observation is needed. Let me ask you. Have you taken a really sharp look around you? Staff complaining to each other in a public setting? Handmade signs? Less than clean bathrooms? Boxes and hand trucks stored visibly in the corner? Posters with bent edges? Dust on the shelves? Furniture torn? Broken web links or outdated web pages? Chipped desks? Customers having to discuss their library bills in public? Out of order signs posted for days on end? Service without a smile? Phones ringing too long? Any one of these issues, while in and of themselves might not be large, signals to the customers that there is a fraying service.

Think for a moment about your own shopping habits. What are the stores that you are attracted to? Bright, well-lit, clean, colorful, neat, well-stocked, and having helpful staff and clear signage are all features that draw us toward certain stores. In short, when we enter these stores, they make a good first impression on us. They transmit a message: good management here.

Without this same message from your library, the image of the service, the library, and you deteriorates. Often, it isn't immediate and it is subtle, but the seed is planted that this library is less than excellent. If you want to be successful at the helm, make sure that the library is always creating a good first impression from the moment that customers first see the library, first walk through the front door, or first interact online.

Of course, that is not enough. Once we secure a good first impression, we have to make sure that the good impression is lasting. What is the best way to ensure a good lasting impression? The answers are old-fashioned but also enduring.

Well, first of all, walk around regularly. Think about one walk around before the library opens. That way, you can look without being distracted. Take a notepad with you to jot down your impressions—you know you aren't going to remember from one area to the next.

Do the second walk around while the library is in full swing. Observe the customers closely and make notes about what you see. And while you are walking around, chat with the staff and interact with the customers.

Walk around every week. Sometimes our days are so busy that we just want to dash to our offices and bury ourselves in the work there. Instead view walking around as any other important task— allot a time for it. Give it priority. If you have branch libraries, department libraries, or bookmobiles, schedule your visits on a regular cycle. You must see your library regularly firsthand.

As part of your regular cycle of assessment of service, include qualitative customer surveys so customers can be encouraged to state their concerns large and small. Of course, you and all supervisors and managers should read their comments in detail.

Consider focus groups. Get together with your customers and ask them questions. Also many libraries hire students. Consider bringing them in for a focus group too. Their front-line experience and straight-talking ways will greatly enlighten any conversation about service. Now if you think that members of any focus group won't speak honestly to you because you are the director, get someone else to moderate the group who will be very good at reporting feedback unfiltered.

Have staff watch the social media—which is an excellent gauge of the immediate reactions of customers. What are your customers saying online about your library? They might be articulating their needs, frustrations, satisfactions, issues, and worries. These informal forums are vital for gathering customer needs.

Have you tried secret shoppers yet? Again, if you are in a university, particularly where there is a graduate program of library studies, a professor might be willing to do this as a class project. Note though, that in spite of the term "secret" shopper, the staff should know and should participate and have a chance to read the results. It might skew the results somewhat when staff are prepared for a secret shopper, but there still will be a wealth of information in the report. Frankly, having a truly secret shopper in a library setting will jeopardize the trust between you and the staff when the news of a real secret shopper gets out—and it will—you already know that libraries are leaky ships in terms of confidential information.

Then, and this is the important step, gather up the notes you took while walking around, the comments from the surveys, focus groups, and various reports; discuss the information with managers, supervisors, and staff as needed; and take action in a thoughtful manner on the feedback. Don't just file the information. Instead work steadily to remove any barriers to creating an ongoing good impression of the library. Otherwise if you don't take action, everyone just becomes frustrated with yet another management process and participation declines. Also, questions arise about your real motivations if the ideas are not turned into action that improves service. The staff will ask each other, "What was the director really up to?" The more you observe the impression the library is making and the more you follow up, the less such questions will arise in the minds of your staff.

Now what if your information gathering startles you with problems that you did not expect? Then it is time to ask yourself some questions. Have you developed a service strategy that has been effectively deployed across the library? Have you instilled the concept of service in your staff? Are they engaged with, trained, and knowledgeable about customer needs? Are you rewarding good service? Are you and other managers and supervisors modeling a commitment toward excellent service and toward making a good impression? Remember staff will respond to a boss's priorities. Staff will focus on what you focus on. You must always transmit your commitment to quality service, to continuous improvement, and to continued correction of problems. If it feels like a perpetual audit, and you find yourself saying, "Didn't we just do that survey?", that is because it is a perpetual audit. The maintenance of quality in any organization is never ending.

> ***Steve Brogden:*** "The one thing every library director should know is the importance of setting a tone at the top, a tone of openness, creativity, and a willingness to experiment. Always look for a way to say yes. If a new program or idea doesn't pan out, laugh about it, chalk it up to experience, and move in a different direction."

Every library director should know that in order to be successful at the helm, good impressions count. All of the effort that you and your staff make behind the scenes to maintaining a quality library will manifest itself when the customers are impressed and delighted with their library experience.

CONTROLLING EXPECTATIONS

The library profession as a whole has a hard time controlling expectations. The problem is built into our profession—the collective number of customers is huge, and their interest in knowledge is infinite. Is it any wonder that we so often have discussions on being all things to all people?

These unchecked expectations come to us in several ways. First, we as librarians add to the problem ourselves. Our extensive networks of communication often mean that we are awash with new ideas. As we just discussed, new ideas flowing in keep our libraries relevant, but who hasn't had the dizzying experience of coming back from a conference both with all of the new things that we want to do and all of the things that we feel guilty about not doing?

Next come the customers. They push forward with expectations of new services and expanded collections. Faculty senate committees, community groups, boards, students, donors and teachers, and many more individuals and groups all want something new or expanded without any realization of the resource costs. This is compounded by the fact that we are a values-driven profession and one of those important values is helping people. We naturally respond to people who want more library services. Who can say no and turn them away?

Lastly come our bosses, and this is a trickier piece. In another chapter, we will talk about bosses, but oftentimes, our bosses will want us to take this or that on. Library directors have high degrees of competence and are willing workers. Is it any wonder that a boss wants us and our libraries to take on more responsibility?

The problem is that if we respond to all of these demands, we may do a lot, but we will not do anything well. You don't and never will have that scale of budget. You don't and never will have enough people to manage a broad scope. You don't and never will have enough time in the work day to manage so many goals. The result is frustration on everyone's part.

So what do you do with this stream of expectations? Keep in mind that management requires a cool head and a steady hand. It is very easy for even an experienced director to be stampeded in the face of some demands.

The way not to get in over your head with expectations is by being very clear about your priorities. These should be clearly artic-ulated in the strategic plan—which should not be a 50-page docu-ment on a shelf—but a short document, referred to frequently, known by everyone, and implemented year after year. New ideas should always be considered in light of what has been agreed upon in the plan. Unless a new idea is very good with an unusual oppor-tunity, don't get sidetracked. It is very easy to bleed energy and resources from your priorities into less important ideas.

Let's talk for a moment about ideas that come to you directly from the customers. Sometimes an individual or small group of customers seek a director out to talk about an idea for library ser-vice. Such customers could be known to you, could be influential, or could simply be a person with an idea. Regardless of the likabil-ity or influence of the customers or the quality of the idea, check any impulse you might have to agree to that idea on the spot even if there is the expressed hope that you will implement the idea imme-diately. Just say thanks and that you will take the matter under advisement. If you agree on the spot to the idea, then you have not done the due diligence necessary for any idea. How does it match up with the strategic plan? What is the recommendation of your staff? Are the resources there? In fact as a result of your quick agreement, you have now contributed to the problem of controlling expectations.

In some situations, you don't even have to commit to following up, which is good because following up presumes you will make a decision. If that decision is no, then you are into a potentially awk-ward conversation. When ideas are presented to you, always keep in mind the culture of librarians—we are so programmed to help that our responses can go to automatic and we find ourselves sud-denly agreeing. Remember you are the director. Your responses are your choices.

Now sometimes an idea may come to you from a customer that is so out of line that you will not give it any further thought. On the spot you have to decide, whether or not you want to tell the customer that the idea is not feasible or whether or not you want to just listen and let it pass. Deciding whether to respond or not will depend upon how aggressive the customer seems. If you reject the idea on the spot, the customer may become more agitated since force begets force. If you think you have one of those people, just thank the customer and make no further comment. Unfortunately people with way out of line ideas are often those who become pests with those ideas. Just remain politely firm each time the request/ suggestion occurs even if it drives you and your staff crazy. One way to reduce your frustration with this situation is to try and see the suggestion through that person's eyes. Sympathy often acts as a brake on annoyance.

Be sure to keep an open mind when hearing ideas though. Even if you are hearing an idea that you have heard many times before, listen anyway and don't cut off the conversation. You never know what new element may be interjected into your thinking. It may be a good enhancement to a current goal. Anyway, it is just good manners and good public relations to listen.

What every library director should know is that one sure way not to succeed in the job is not to deliver. We cannot deliver on every expectation that everyone has of our libraries. Trying to be all things to all people is a recipe for disaster.

DOWNSTREAM THINKING

We all know that every problem opens up a chance for opportunity and a chance for disaster. Additionally, while most problems have solutions, solutions themselves can create problems further down the road. Problem solving, especially of any magnitude, is tricky business.

Our ability to solve problems, regardless of their source, lies in our capability to do downstream thinking, which means the capability to see the consequences of our actions. We have all seen a river flow. It winds downstream sometimes roughly, sometimes smoothly, but sooner or later we cannot see it after it bends. And the trouble always lies beyond the bend.

Fortunately, human beings have a wonderful capability—it is called the ability to simulate. While we might not be able to see where the water flows, we can simulate it in our minds based upon our prior experiences and knowledge. Therefore, when considering every decision or action, take a moment both alone and with the staff and simulate what will happen downstream if such and such a solution was implemented. Fully simulating, that is living out the experience, will tell you a lot about how successful the solution will be.

Simulating using downstream thinking is an important way to avoid unintended consequences, which can be very serious—all the more so because sometimes around-the-bend problems don't show up for a while. Moreover, staff might not tell you immediately about negative consequences of a decision because they don't want to be the messenger. This brings us to our next point.

THE CONSPIRACY OF SILENCE

Beware of the conspiracy of silence. You may have grown up in this library and have deep contacts and connections, but you are now the boss and communication is significantly altered by power. You know how hard it is for people to speak truth to power. Library directors have to be very aware that the full truth may not come or may come too late. The performance of an individual, a struggling service, a budget concern, a significant safety issue can all be reported but often softened. People are aware that the messenger is often killed. No one really likes to hear bad news after all.

How can you overcome the conspiracy of silence? Well, you won't ever be able to overcome it completely. However, establishing an environment which is trusting and open is the best way to minimize this issue. Make it safe for people to come forward—not just to you but to all of the supervisors.

How do you make it safe? Frankly, just appreciate people who are willing to deliver the bad news. If you have an upset look on your face or you explode in frustration or anger when you hear bad news, no one will want to come forward. If you talk about the person afterward in bad tones or avoid them in the future for being negative, no one will want to come forward. If you ding them in a performance evaluation for such things as attitude, no one will want to come forward again. Remember that people are not fooled. They respond both to our language, our subtle cues, and our behavior. If you want to break the conspiracy of silence, encourage talking in a friendly and safe environment.

TARGET FIXATION

Target fixation is a process whereby the brain becomes so fixed on an object that other objects or hazards diminish. Take fighter pilots as an example. Sometimes a pilot becomes so fixated on the target that he or she misses something big like the ground or a mountain.

It is a very relevant concept to management. Sometimes we become so fixed on a single issue that we don't see the bigger issue around it.

Target fixation can also lead to confirmation blindness. Sometimes we become fixated on a solution to the exclusion of all other options.

In short, we are narrowing our field of vision. Instead of seeing the whole picture, we are very focused on a smaller section of it. When a director loses the broad perspective, there is always danger because we may miss lurking problems, trouble spots, or better options. How can you keep a broad perspective?

First, identify the real problem. A lot of times problems will be presented to you but the real problem lies somewhere underneath that. Don't be in a hurry and rush the employee along just because the problem sounds like something you have heard before. Listen fully to what the employee has to say. Have time and tolerance to understand the issue and uncover the real problem. In short, broaden your understanding.

Always look at a range of solutions. Don't stay fixed on one solution. You will find an optimum solution but rarely one solution only. After all, this is management not mathematics. Be sure to test the possible solutions on staff, and perhaps customers, and get feedback.

Do take time for mature deliberation. Very rarely must a decision be rushed. Usually there is time to think about the solutions presented. Mature deliberation is essentially the old "sleep on it overnight" idea. Things do look different in the morning as the brain continues to process the problem and may present new ideas and solutions. Don't be in a hurry but give the solution time to mature in your mind and in the minds of others.

Finally, watch who has what agenda. Remember that individuals may be pushing either a problem or a solution because of a hidden agenda. Hidden agendas are never in the best interest of the library as a whole. Talk to everyone who has a stake in the problem and in the solution. Continue to have a healthy dose of skepticism about both the problem and the solution. A skillful director believes nothing without casting a critical eye over any issue.

Be cautious about internal and external forces that narrow your perspective because a narrow perspective seriously affects your judgment on any issue.

THE LONG DISTANCE RUNNER

Short bursts of speed are fine for most projects but the successful library director has to be a long distance runner. The achievement of long-term goals and strategies requires a steady application of attention, work, and focus. Will that goal really take three years to complete? So what? Will it really take two years to dismiss a problem employee? So what, again? What is important is the achievement of the goal not the time it takes.

The trouble is that many times we lose steam when pursuing long-term goals. The energy, motivation, and focus to fulfill the long-term goals become dissipated over time. This is why so many strategic plans are never achieved and why people roll their eyes when they think about strategic planning.

The bottom line? You can't lose your energy toward long-term goals. You can't drift. If you want to achieve long-term goals, many of which are the most important that the library will ever undertake, you have to be a long distance runner. You have to stay on track and keep going toward your goals no matter what the effort or time.

Elizabeth Martinez: The one thing that every library director should know is . . . "to evaluate and access and provide services based on a public perspective (as opposed to a professional). The library belongs to the people of the community; we are the custodians of the library for the residents/students, and [the library is] customized and transformed for each community."

THE MASTER OF INTEGRATION

You may have been one of the finest catalogers ever, but that isn't your job anymore. You may have been a whiz at information research, but that isn't your job either. Once you accept a director position, you have given up those specializations. It doesn't mean you aren't interested, but it cannot be the focus of your attention. Now, people will tell you that you have moved from being a specialist to being a generalist. Don't you believe it—you have a new specialty. You must now be the master of integration.

Unlike some corporations, libraries don't have multiple lines of business. In fact, we really just have one business—connecting the customer to knowledge. As a result, a library has to be highly managed because it is an integrated whole. This means that you, as the director, have the final responsibility for integrating all of the systems. If you make a decision regarding reference, it likely will affect technical services. If you make a decision relating to circulation, it likely will affect reference, and so on. Your job is to make those connections. You have to continually view the library as a single system.

If you keep in mind the library as a single integrated system, it will help you to avoid some costly mistakes. As a director, you will of course make mistakes—less as you mature in experience but still mistakes will occur. However, you can only afford a few errors before the staff loses confidence. One error that you definitely want to avoid is making a decision that optimizes one area at the cost of another. In other words, the losing service is suboptimized. When you suboptimize a service, it is a clear message that you do not understand that service or don't care. Worse, staff assume that you favor one department over another. As a master of integration, it is your job to understand the impact of your decisions on the total systems of the library.

The best way to avoid this error is by talking to everyone who is affected by the decision. Let them know what you are thinking, get their feedback and pay attention to it. This is one of the main reasons that we don't make decisions alone or only with the same people. Get the relevant people involved. Take your blinders off and understand the consequences of your decisions and its impact on the library as a whole.

THE PROOF IS IN THE PUDDING

Everyone is familiar with the slang phrase, "The proof is in the pudding." It means that regardless of the quality of the chefs, the nature of the ingredients, or the recipe carefully followed, the true test of the pudding is in the taste itself.

The same is true of library service. The true test of the quality of service is in its taste—that is, the reaction of the customers to it. Perhaps all the ingredients were there but were they mixed to the liking of the customers? Now you might be "making the pudding" to the taste of your boss, but the boss will still end up judging you by the satisfaction of your customers. Upset customers eventually will mean an upset boss.

The bottom line here is that you never want to take your eyes off the customers or off their changing needs. Remember that when you became a library director, you entered into an unwritten contract with the customers. You are there to take care of their information and knowledge needs. You are there to enable their advancement. The customers are one of the most important reasons for your existence as a director.

Whenever you make a decision, always ask yourself this question—what is best for our customers? How will this decision help our customers? What will be our customers' reaction to this decision? You must see them in your mind's eye continually standing in front of you and be concerned about their needs all day long. The customers are the final judge of the library.

Sandra G. Yee: "Never underestimate the power of the position! Early in my career as dean, my associate dean kindly reminded me that this is an awesome thing. When a dean

speaks, staff members listen, and try to follow. When a dean
asks that something be done, staff members attempt to do it.
What this means is that along with the power comes a huge
responsibility to always set an example of high integrity, honesty, and hard work, all the while giving credit to staff members where it is due and encouraging everyone to follow your
lead. Be the leader they want to follow and you will be successful!"

THE LIBRARIAN-IN-CHIEF

There must be thousands of articles and books written on leadership—what it is, how it works, how to be good at it, how it is
different from management. This is not the place for that discussion, so let's get to the bottom line. As the library director, you
have to be a leader and a manager and a follower. As a leader, you
have to set the vision, the values, and the directions for the library.
As a manager, you have to deploy the resources and strategies to
deliver that vision. As a follower, you have to be good support not
only to your boss but also to your own staff.

Here is the strategic issue. Don't get so caught up in the day to
day that you lose sight of the vision. Don't get so caught up in your
vision that you lack practicality about delivery. Don't get so caught
up in following others that you unintentionally abdicate your position.

In short, you are juggling these three roles continually. Your
success depends upon your ability to know which role is important
and when. We all have heard directors accused of being microman-
agers. That is largely the result of lacking focus on the vision or the
big picture. We have all heard of directors being accused of being
"flaky." That is largely the result of lacking focus on deliverables.
We have all heard of directors being accused of weakness. As often
as not, that is the result of a director that has not stepped up to the

leadership role. What every library director should know is the importance of moving skillfully and deliberately between these roles in order to be effective at the helm of the library.

CONCLUSION

Think upon these strategies from time to time. They will help you at the helm of the library. Don't just read them once and then move on but instead let the ideas mature and gel in your mind. As you work through your day, consider these strategies and their implications for your actions.

Chapter Two

Customer Number One: Your Boss

It scarcely needs to be said that the entire focus of librarianship is on the customers. Our library education and our careers point entirely toward having satisfied and happy customers. Our facilities, our resources, and our services are about their needs and their comfort.

Therefore, this chapter heading may be surprising for there is a number one customer before all other customers. Customer Number One is your boss. Think about it this way. Your boss pays your salary. True, the funds might come from a governmental or other source, but the boss is the one who determines your salary and determines your raises. Your boss writes your performance review. Your boss has the power to hire and fire you or even to transfer you or reduce you to another level. Equally important is the fact that the boss determines the budget you receive for the library. Yes, there may be other funding mechanisms that determine the budget but the role of the boss is critical. Therefore, the boss has significant power over both your professional life and the life of your library.

Therefore, what every library director should know is that it is imperative to view the boss as customer number one. This chapter focuses on what it takes to be successful with your boss.

LIVING THE CONTEXT

As library directors, we live within several worlds. We live in the world of the librarian profession. We live in the world of the organization that is the parent to the library. We also live in the world of the boss. Therefore, just as we keep up with our profession by knowing its trends and issues and just as we keep up with the parent organization by knowing what's happening, we also need to keep up with the context within which the boss dwells.

Understanding the context of a boss is vital to working successfully with the boss. Understanding the viewpoint, the stresses, and the priorities of the boss helps us to work with him or her. When you want to propose a new project to your boss, doesn't it help if you know the boss's priorities? When you are requesting additional funds, doesn't it help to know what strain your boss' budget is already under? When you are bringing a problem to be solved, doesn't it help to know if that week has been particularly stressful for the boss?

What is important here is to make a study of the boss. The same way that you study the customers to get to know their needs, you have to study your boss. Many of us do this instinctively, but I am asking you to take this to a more conscious level. Think about the individual, the personality, the likes and dislikes, the orientation to work, the worries, the major issues, the conflicts, and the politics under which the boss lives. In other words, develop a deep understanding of the world in which your boss lives. You might feel that this is too manipulative, but is it? Organizational life requires endless strategy to get your library to where you want it to be.

If your boss is the mayor (or a similar position, for there are many variations), you have an additional dimension to understanding the context of the boss. You must view your work through the political lens of your boss. Many mayors want to be reelected and many aspire to higher political office, therefore their eye is always on the polls. Even those who are at career end want to assure their legacy. When you are engaged in major change or a controversy is brewing, always look at the issue with a political eye. What will be the impact on the public? What will be the headlines?

It is not as easy to understand the boss's context as we might think. We may know a lot, but we also have not been in the private conversations, not attended all of the boss's meetings, nor had the responsibilities, pressures, and worries that come with the higher level. Therefore, never make the assumption that you know every-thing about your boss. Think about yourself. Does your staff really know all about you?

One approach to work that might give you a surprising level of understanding and even more compassion for the challenges of the boss's job is to work as if you were your boss. Always keep before you the concept of "completed work." This is work that is done as if you were at the next level up. So do your work as if your boss were doing it. Not only will the boss recognize this and deeply appreciate it (after all, then it becomes less work for him or her) but it will help you to continually think in the boss's frame of mind.

BUCKING THE BOSS

Bucking the boss means going against the boss overtly or covertly. Another slang term could be "taking the boss on." One would think that common sense or just plain survival instincts would curb peo-ple's intentions about bucking the boss. Professionally, it certainly is suicidal behavior in any organization. However, I have seen it happen throughout my career. Let's take a look at how to avoid bucking the boss, which, by the way, usually has a bad ending for the library director.

First of all, let's look at the attitudes that get us to bucking the boss. There seem to be two attitudes within a person that create this situation. Arrogance is one cause. Arrogance means that you feel better than and superior to the boss. It might of course be true that you do have more talent and ability, but arrogance always back-fires.

Arrogance often stems from two sources. The first is ignorance of the boss's capabilities. Think about it this way: the boss did have what it took to get to that job and has what it takes to keep it. Is it possible that you have underestimated the boss's abilities? The second source of arrogance is overconfidence. Again, you might be very talented, but as a director it is very important to constantly have a reality check on your own abilities. Are you 100 percent sure that you are better? Do you think your talents have been tested with the same challenges that the boss's talents have been tested?

Another attitude that can get us to bucking the boss is anger if the boss has failed to meet our expectations. For example, we may get mad or revengeful when the boss does not give us the raise we wanted or if we see that others, more recently hired or with less responsibility, are getting more money. Perhaps we are not getting the recognition that we want or should have. Perhaps we are not in the inner circle of the boss and feel alienated. All of these can lead to anger. Just remember that the boss does not have to meet your expectations. Instead, the boss has to meet the expectations of his or her own boss. You also have to realize that anger can eventually be detected, which may increase the sense of distance between you and the boss.

Now with that understanding, let's look at the ways to avoid bucking the boss.

First of all, don't jump the line, which means that you don't go over the boss's head ever. You don't go to your boss's boss to discuss issues or concerns which are rightly the domain of your boss. Never forget that organizations are tribal, that is, there is a chief and there are the rest of us aligned in a hierarchy. Be under no illusions—all organizations have an iron fist in a velvet glove. To jump the line creates deep anger in the boss because it means that you do not have respect for or confidence in the boss. It also is a direct threat to the power and job security of the boss. After all, if you are going over the boss's head, it isn't because you want to deliver words of praise.

Now sometimes, particularly in organizations that might be more casually run, your boss may invite you to let his or her higher up know about such and such an issue. That's okay as long as you make sure that you keep your boss in the loop by copying the boss on any communication or by informing the boss later. This invitation by the boss means that you are trusted—that is, trusted not to do the boss in.

Never give ultimatums. People who give ultimatums to their boss have no sense of their role in the organization and how easily expendable they are. Do we really think that bosses got where they did because they could be intimidated? So phrases such as "if I don't get this raise, I am going to walk" or "this budget has to increase or I am finding another position" will likely get you on the street or transferred elsewhere—if not immediately then not long after. Remember bosses have time on their side and can wait to make a move just when we think we might have them cornered. You might think that you are exercising power and showing them who is the boss, but this is a very serious misunderstanding of your own power—or lack of it. When you give an ultimatum, you enter into a power struggle with your boss—and even if you could win—which is a remote chance—you look bad in front of everyone else especially other bosses who now brand you as a problem employee.

When people have not been in the corridors of power, they don't always understand the real power of a boss. They think they can not only take on but also defeat a boss. Now, I have seen bosses hounded out of their jobs, but it is an uncommon and rare occurrence. More often than not, it ends in disaster for the employee. Remember that a boss has access to more powerful people and the boss's words will count for more than yours. This is especially true if the boss is politically well connected. What are the clues to the well connected? Pay attention if you learn that your boss spends his or her off time with other upper managers. Are they golfing together? Shopping together? Lunching often? Do they have "in" jokes? These are all small indicators that the boss may be better connected than you think.

Never bad-mouth the boss. Oh, I know it is tempting sometimes when you are very frustrated and annoyed. There are two considerations here. The first consideration is a question of character. We should be respectful of people and this includes the individual for whom you work. Common decency should prevail here. Listen to yourself when you are bad-mouthing someone. Is that really the person you want to be? Importantly, is that the role model that you want to be for your own staff?

The second consideration is a practical matter. After all, even if your boss is not the one who hired you, the boss is the one who is keeping you on the job. Does it really make sense to bite the hand that feeds you?

Watch out for people who you think are your buddies when you bad-mouth the boss to them. Remember people are trying to rise in an organization and you have just given them something that can be used to further their ambitions. Gossip is a bonding device. If you tell someone something that is damaging about the boss, that person, ruthless and ambitious, could easily repeat to the boss what you have said. Of course, your comments would be recrafted in such a way as to give the boss a "heads up" on potential problems (that would be you). The goal of this mischief maker is to be appreciated by the boss as someone who transmits valuable insider information.

Be careful when people try to lure you into these types of conversations. This is dangerous ground. We can get quite comfortable in organizations especially if we have been there for a long time but we should never view organizations as completely safe places. You have only yourself to blame if your harsh words get back to the boss. And we all know that words once spoken cannot be taken back. Your boss will remember.

Finally, one great challenge is when the boss gives you a goal and you really disagree with it. You might be tempted to buck this, but you already know that is not the solution. Instead, go in this sequence: First, weigh how important it is to your boss. Is this something that means a lot to your boss? Try to really understand the goal. Sometimes, because our bosses are not in our profession and don't have our lingo, they might express themselves in a way that isn't exactly how we would understand it. So first, when confronted with an unlikable goal, do seek understanding. It might not be as bad as you think. However, if it is, then you have to do your best, without being annoying, to persuade your boss otherwise. This might not be something that you want to do on the spot when the idea is first shared, because it would seem, and in fact, would be, confrontational. Instead, ask the boss if you could think about it for a bit and then get back to him or her. That later time is when you discuss your concerns and also your suggested modifications to the goal. Your modifications might be something you both can live with.

Now of course sometimes the idea is really appalling and you know you will have a problem on your hands. Worse, you have to go back and tell the staff. Here is where it is tempting to say that the boss is forcing you into this and you don't agree with it or want to do it. This can be accompanied by rolling your eyes. Put the brakes on before you go into this direction. First, if the staff thinks you are being forced into something that you really disagree with, you look weak, as if you have no influence over the boss, and this is never good for your long-term management of the library. Second, continue to remember that you are also modeling behavior. You might get eye rolling too one of these days, and why not, since after all, you have already shown that it is acceptable. Instead, present the goal, explain its priority to the boss, show the boss's reasoning behind the goal and acknowledge the challenges. Let people whine but not too long. Be matter of fact. Don't be negative, but you don't have to be a "company boy or girl" either.

It is important to state openly here the tried and true strategy of stalling. No one likes to mention this in the open, but in fact, stalling is often deployed. Confronted with a goal that makes no sense, it is not uncommon for a director to simply stall. Here, a director is gambling that the boss will forget or move onto other things. That way, there will not be obvious bucking of the directives. While it seems Machiavellian, it might be better than taking on a disastrous goal. Of course, the trick is not to get caught stalling. Failing to fulfill the boss's stated goals can end up easily in a very awkward conversation and finally in a performance review.

The bottom line on this is to be the staff member you wish you had. Would you really want someone who bucks you, is disloyal, bad-mouths you, and goes over your head? Of course not. In fact, you would want to get rid of that individual.

BEING TOUGH WITH YOURSELF

Every boss wants a good employee that comes to work, gets the job done, and minimizes the demand on the boss's time. There are also emotions and behaviors that we don't realize that we are engaging in that are very annoying to any boss. Let's take a look at these.

First of all, stop complaining about the workload. You are paid that salary with the expectation that you will work hard and take on a lot of responsibility. Complaining about the workload is another way of saying "look at me," "look at how valuable I am." This becomes very fatiguing to everyone around you. Most of all eliminate from your comments that you work 60 hours every week. You really don't work 60 hours a week. That is 8.5 hours a day, *seven* days a week. Yes, there will be some weeks here and there when you do, but it shouldn't be routine, and if it is, there may be something wrong with how you are conducting your job. Take a harsh look at yourself and see if you have become a micromanager. Your boss certainly will be taking a look if you complain often enough, because the message to the boss is that you can't handle the job.

Remember that the boss's priorities are your priorities. If the boss needs something done, do it in spite of your other priorities. Be careful not to have this annoying conversation with your boss: Sometimes when we are really on overload and the boss gives us a project, it is tempting to have a meeting with the boss and ask the boss to prioritize this new project against your other priorities. You think you are being a skillful and thoughtful manager by asking the boss's help in prioritizing. The boss thinks you are dodging the project. And the boss is right. Is your motivation for this conversation really about prioritizing the work? Or is it really about trying to take some of the workload off your plate? Always keep in mind that no boss cares about your workload or about how you accomplish your work—just get it done right and on time.

A boss gets sick of hearing people whine. Yes, the budget is bad; yes, the library hasn't been recarpeted in twenty years; yes, facility maintenance is lousy; yes, yes, yes. Just stop it. Unless these are things your boss can or will change, just let it go and stop being a broken record. Start focusing on the positive things that are being accomplished. Remember attitude matters a ton. Bosses are like anyone else. They like to be around positive people too.

Forget about excuses with your boss. You didn't get to something or deliver on something because of this and that excuse. The boss isn't really interested in that. Now maybe there is a genuine reason why you failed to do something but you should have been talking to the boss all along and not at the end. When you start making excuses, you just look bad, and worse, you look weak, as if everything is out of your control. Along that line, never pass the buck. If you are in charge, whatever happens in the library is your responsibility. It isn't the fault of your staff, or the resources, or another unit on campus. It is your job. Step up to your position.

Don't be frustrated if the boss doesn't remember everything you do. It can be annoying when you have to refresh the boss's mind several times, but think about the scope of the boss's work. He or she has a lot of direct reports with many decisions, actions, and issues all day long. The mind of the boss is crowded with activities. Honestly, do you remember everything that everyone in the library is doing?

When you need your boss's decision on issues, come with several possible solutions. Don't just come with the problem. Now it might be that the problem is beyond your experience, but the boss will appreciate that you have some suggestions and alternatives. Try to keep control of solving your own problems.

Be mindful of timing. If you know your boss has had a hard week or a long day, is that a time to bring forward a packet of problems? If your boss is leaving for vacation or for a long weekend, is that the time to present a serious issue? Yes, of course, you have to bring emergency issues to the boss's attention but otherwise, be aware of timing. Remember too that if your timing is off and your boss is rushed or exhausted, you might not get a good decision, or worse, you might get a decision with which you don't want to live. Additionally, when you leave the boss's office, you want the boss to have a pleasant feeling toward you not a feeling of annoyance or frustration. And by the way, don't ever ask for a meeting on a Friday afternoon. That is the time that the boss wants to leave early after an exhausting week or wrap up some lingering projects in order to go home with a clear mind.

Careful about overstepping your boundaries. Sometimes, especially when we are new to a position, we don't always know exactly what our boundaries are so we might take actions that actually belong to the boss. No boss appreciates a staff member in his or her territory—this is a direct threat to power. Some examples of the territory of the boss might include very large purchases, political issues that deal with the boss's boss, serious problem employees, and so forth.

Accept criticism graciously. Nobody likes to be criticized and this gets tougher as you become more senior in your work. After all, you got there because you have high levels of competence. But if you are in this situation, accept it graciously. Try to understand the boss, try to see the perspective, try to look for solutions, and then say thank you for pointing this out and helping you. Giving criticism is very tough on a boss also, and any boss will appreciate it if you ease the situation by accepting the criticism graciously and maturely. Moreover, you might actually learn something.

And what about kissing up? This is one of the most disliked behaviors. The boss may enjoy it for a while, but any boss worth anything sees through it shortly. There are two dangers with kissing up: first, you can become an object of ridicule to the boss and to peers. Second, peers who witness this behavior also find it threatening because it might mean that you are rising in power. So this triggers covert action to help bring you down. Now this doesn't mean you should not praise the boss legitimately. After all, bosses rarely get honest praise from staff so they do enjoy it, but kissing up shows that you are willing to sacrifice your own dignity just to get ahead. Of course, the sad part of this is that we all know people who did get ahead by kissing up. Usually it is because they linked to a boss who was seduced by flattery and who wanted "yes men" not managers. It is a sorry career though.

No matter what, if you want to work effectively with Customer Number One, the best course of action that every library director should know is to step up to the job, be mature, and be responsible.

MARKET YOURSELF

You do have to be in the business of marketing yourself, which is hard for some who are naturally humble. Generally speaking, we are not in a profession full of showboats. But if you don't market yourself, you will be invisible to the boss and you won't get where you need to go.

Now, you might say, that you don't want to rise to higher positions in the organization. You don't want to be a provost, a principal, a city manager, and so on. Okay, but you do want to rise in power, which helps you both personally and helps your library very much.

As you think about marketing yourself to your boss, take this into consideration. As a director, you embody the library. You are the most public symbol of the library. While you will have individual accomplishments, such as writing a great article or being elected to professional office, most of your achievements are the achievements of the library as a whole. When the library looks good, you also look good.

So when I say market yourself to your boss, make your individual accomplishments as well as the accomplishments of your library visible. The two are intertwined, although marketing the library isn't easy. Many of the true achievements of a library are impossible to explain outside of the profession or lack the glamor factor. This is why our profession seems to be in endless justification. We will always struggle with this. We often don't get the respect we deserve because people really cannot understand what it is we do all day long—let alone what those achievements are. Moreover, never think that when your boss says that the library is the "heart" of the university, the city, or the school that your library is well marketed. These phrases are just public comments and little more than lip service.

This does not mean that we give up. Take a look around you at what other units in the parent organization are sharing with your boss. What do they celebrate? Grants? Research? Community relations? Awards? Major gifts? Keep on the hunt all the time for achievements that will be good to celebrate and of course understandable outside of the library profession. This isn't a once-a-year event: marketing must go on year-round. You and the library can never afford to be invisible. Constantly your boss must be aware of all of the good things that are going on and the good work that your staff is doing. The library should be a continual source of pride. Remember this also makes the boss look good and gives your boss desirable talking points.

A library is a natural centerpiece of an organization. Many libraries are physically beautiful: true showcases that are a point of prestige. Additionally, libraries evoke good emotions because of the respect that many have for the value of knowledge and the appreciation that many have for our kind service. Play this role up with your boss. Continually offer the library as a center for guests, events, speakers, and exhibits that are important to your boss who will appreciate your participation and support. This strategy also keeps the library in the forefront of your boss's thinking, because he or she will be continually walking through your front door and speaking positively about your library to the guests.

Form alliances with the public relations department. Almost every parent organization will have a PR department. Give them some moving stories and let the professionals do the marketing for you. They are always looking for good stories, and it will be very useful for you to be known as a good source for quotes or stories.

Now, one advantage that libraries have is a wide range of customers, including kids, with great public interest stories. Have your customers speak for you. They also can be a great source for quotes and photos. Of course, this has to be managed so you don't have wild card in the pack.

While marketing yourself is vital, make sure that you are not the hero of every story. This is a great chance to give your boss an

However, when coming up to speak with the boss's boss, don't avoid the other little guy who is already there speaking with him or her. Have you yet had the experience of speaking to someone powerful and another person comes up and doesn't even acknowledge your existence? It is a funny thing about power—it makes everyone else invisible.

Remember too that speaking to the boss's boss is an opportunity to praise your boss. It is not an opportunity to run down or criticize your boss. First of all, it will get back to your boss. Second, it makes you look bad; it is important to be classy and respectful.

Don't think though, no matter how many witty stories you tell, that you will become part of the boss's boss in crowd. You won't. There is a dividing line between you called the organizational hierarchy, so don't get desperate. Just know who you are and continue to do the best job you can.

RELATING EFFECTIVELY

Considering that we spend most of our lives in organizations reporting to a boss, it is surprising how naïve we can be about it sometimes. This section goes over some of the common mistakes that we make in relating to a boss.

First, don't expect more than the boss can give. Organizations are not families. Often people misunderstand organizations deeply and believe the hype about being one family that supports each other. It is very important to have your eyes wide open about what an organization really is. You should never be under any illusion how fast your bags can be packed and how fast you can be out the door.

Certainly, people in organizations can act with tremendous compassion and understanding. Bonds, sometimes lifelong bonds, are forged and deep friendships made. However always be aware that the director's job is to serve the purposes of the organization according to the directions of the boss and when that ceases, so does the director's job.

Never surprise your boss. If you want to get him or her angry, this is a surefire way. Blindsiding any boss with information that he or she should have had all along is suicidal. When a boss is caught by surprise, it is a direct threat to power and prestige especially if the surprise comes in public. Think about how you feel when you are caught by surprise. It looks as if you do not know what is going on in your own organization. Communicate effectively all the time on issues but don't overdo it. A boss doesn't want to hear from the library director every day. Communication must be selective and relevant.

> ***Marsha Kmec***: What every library director should know is . . . "the absolute necessity for full and open communication with your patrons and most importantly: administration. Today's library director must be a communication extrovert to ensure that the evolving and dynamic needs of his or her host facility and its patrons are anticipated, met, and exceeded— often before they are even expressed. There is no substitute for regular, in-person communication to optimize the delivery of exceptional service."

A moment more on communication: do get to know the boss's preferred style of communication. Perhaps the boss only wants to meet in person on major mission-critical issues or prefers detail in writing or prefers to hear most issues in person. The more you understand the boss's communication style, the better chance you have of getting your message across.

Tell the boss only the minimum of personal information. This is a workplace not a therapy session or a confessional. The longer we are in organizations, or the longer we work for one person, the more we come to share confidences and the more we let our guard down. Family arguments, marital disagreements, illnesses that have no impact on work—all of these things are not matters for a boss. Remember that you have to give the boss confidence that you are capable, competent, and in control. Some personal information flies right in the face of that. Leave it at home. Guard against your own vulnerability.

Now it happens sometimes that you are personal friends with your boss. You might have risen in the organization together or perhaps through the chemistry that happens between people you have just become friends. This is always a bit tricky. Your boss, and also your friend, has to make decisions regarding the library. Your boss will have to review your performance and make decisions about your salary increases or merit bonuses. Don't take the boss's decisions personally if the decisions go against you. Remember that your boss has a role to play and a career to build.

Now, while a friendship with the boss is usually to your advantage you must be very careful never to take advantage. Two things can make the boss rightly suspect that you are using the friendship to advantage yourself—either can end the friendship. One is tearing down others who might be giving you problems; the second is talking about/showing off your friendship to others. Frankly, it will become known anyway that you and the boss are friends because others are also watching the boss. Do be aware that a friendship between you and boss always awakens that powerful emotion— jealousy—which so often is at the root of so much mischief between peers. Also be aware that peers will be simultaneously friendlier and more cautious toward you since you now are connected to power. It is a kind of reflected glory that might go to your head and give you a false impression of your standing in the organization. The best approach when you are friends with your boss is simply to keep an even keel and be a true friend.

Never share whom you like and dislike in an organization. When you are asked to work with someone, it is irrelevant if you like or don't like them. You work with everyone. If not, you face the possibility that the boss begins to see you as a target for what is wrong. No boss needs more headaches, and if you reveal an inability to get along with this or that person, you are creating more headaches. Think about how tired you get negotiating the shoals of who will work with whom in your library.

Always remember that what you say to the boss's secretary, you say to the boss. A good secretary is loyal to the boss and therefore considers it necessary to report to the boss what is being said. If there is something that you want to say to the boss but not directly, then a good secretary is a good conduit. The risk here of course is that the secretary may also transmit his/her misunderstandings or bias to the boss as well. Now if you have a mindless moment and complain to the secretary about the boss or are upset about an issue relating to the boss, that information likely will go to the boss too. Always keep in mind that while a good secretary often will discriminate in the information provided to the boss, an important part of a secretary's role is to give the boss a head's up as to the mood of the workplace.

It is important to act indispensable, but underneath don't be surprised if you are not. To act indispensable is an act of power both in terms of how you feel about your job and the message that you transmit to others. After all, you cannot walk around scared that this is your last day—how effective would one be then? But never be surprised if you are not indispensable. I have seen people with exceptional competence and dedication here today and gone tomorrow. One should always have awareness of this possibility.

Unfortunately, when serious trouble is brewing, it is often the lieutenants that are sacrificed. If you are caught up with your boss in a political situation, don't be surprised if you are the one who goes while the boss stays. This is particularly true if you report to a mayor/elected officials and the public is calling for blood.

Sometimes your boss will ask you to take on new responsibilities outside of the library. That is not a time to say, "That is not my job." Even if it seems to you that this new responsibility should lie elsewhere, when your boss says it is your job, then it is your job. Yes, you have a job description and you know what a library director does, but in the end, your boss tells you what your job is. Remember that your boss is undoubtedly trying to solve a problem through this reassignment of responsibilities and will not appreciate it if you don't help out. Of course, don't be so flattered to be asked that you forget to negotiate for a higher salary and/or a new title if the new responsibility is big enough.

THE BOOSTER

One of the many traits that managers share is a positive attitude about the organization. Managers speak positively about the organization's directions, support its goals, and praise its actions and achievements. Any managers who are worth their salt will be boosters of the organization. In order to relate effectively to your boss, and your boss's boss, be an organizational booster too. The same way that you are a booster for your own library, you should also be a booster for the parent organization whether it is a corporation, school, university, city, museum, armed forces, and so on.

Again, it is an understanding of context. Your boss is a large and powerful part of the parent organization or may even be the head of the organization. Likely, the professional identity of your boss has become linked to the success of the organization. Anyway, just from a survival viewpoint, how long will any manager last who doesn't believe in the organization or who speaks negatively about it? There really is no place for negativity in an organization. Negativity sends a message of unhappiness in the workplace. An unhappy attitude is not conducive to having a future with the organization.

Your boss will enjoy that you are a booster too. Every boss enjoys being around a positive employee who shares the same views and attitudes and who celebrates the organization's achievements. Also, don't forget that to praise the organization is to praise the boss because your boss probably had a very large hand in those achievements.

This doesn't mean that you have to gush every time something happens. That will never ring true. This doesn't mean that you have to be the number one cheerleader either—others can take on that role—but do make an effort to applaud a job well done. Speak positively about events, look forward to change, see the future as bright. Never forget to congratulate people on accomplishments. Praising others does not diminish us. Don't we like it when someone says, "Well done!"

Do link the successes and directions of the library to the organization's directions and successes. This doesn't mean that you are always saying "me, too," but look for solid and visible opportunities to show how the library is contributing to the larger enterprise of the parent organization. Don't assume that anyone outside of the library will make that link without your prompting.

Be a booster and a good citizen of whatever organization you are in.

BAD BOSSES

Very few of us escape bad bosses in our careers. However, most bosses are not truly bad but instead are on a spectrum of ability. Some just don't have the skill set for the job. Others don't have the personality—perhaps not really a people person. Others don't have the energy for it. Some cannot bear conflict. Some waffle too much with decisions. Some are too selfish. Any one of these problems can earn a person a reputation as a bad boss because the staff becomes very frustrated over time with such weaknesses in skills or behavior.

Let's look at some strategies in dealing with a bad boss.

First, back to boss analysis; try to understand what your concern really is with your boss. What are the traits or behaviors of your boss that really concern you? Sometimes naming and identifying the specifics that are annoying you can help to demystify what is occurring.

Next, look at your own reactions. In your mind, simulate your action/reaction to your boss. When the boss does this or that, what do you do? Understanding the boss's traits and your reaction helps you to develop a plan of action and helps you to control your behavior in response. In truth, you cannot control the boss's behavior, but you certainly can control your own. Watch your own behavior very carefully and don't develop a hair trigger every time the boss engages in behavior that annoys the heck out of you. Instead be rational in your response.

> ***Virginia Walter***: What every library director should know is . . . "her own strengths, weaknesses, and biases."

For example, say that your boss doesn't listen well and you never have time to get your point across before being cut off. You might be leaving the boss's office continually frustrated. Perhaps in that case, have just a few lines that you want to say and either transmit before the meeting or follow up later with a report with more detail.

Or another example, perhaps your boss is weak in decision making. Rather than walking out of the office, muttering to yourself that you can never get an answer, give the boss a couple of options and say, "If it's okay with you, we'll go in that direction." In short, you would take charge of decision making.

Be careful not to magnify the problem. Don't make it bigger than it is. Every manager has strengths and weaknesses. We are fortunate if we know what they are.

Instead, of focusing on the boss's most annoying traits, focus on the boss's expectations. This leads us away from emotional reactions to reasoned assessment and directions. In every frustrating exchange with your boss, think What is the goal here? What is the expectation?

Of course, there are truly bad bosses—egocentric, arrogant, dictatorial, unethical, cruel, or with disturbing personality disorders. Some engage in questionable activities that may be illegal. Ironically, sometimes truly bad bosses do rise to power and sometimes can keep jobs for a long time—even routinely get promoted.

There are no happy solutions to working with a truly bad boss. If it looks like the bad boss is going to be there for the long run, and that is hard to predict, you might want to consider another position. Often for family, pensions, or other reasons however, we cannot leave our jobs and have no choice except to stay. In that case, keep your head down and do the job. Remember that other people also are experiencing this person as a bad boss and there may be a cumulative effect, the disgust of so many people over time, to bring this individual down. There may also be, at last, the awakening of the boss's boss to the problem. However that can take a very long time especially if your bad boss is friends with his or her boss. Engage in your own survival during this time.

Be careful not to join a hunting party. What is a hunting party? It is a group of people who out of desperation ban together to bring a boss down. A hunting party does not take direct action such as reporting the boss to the boss's boss or to human relations but instead takes indirect action such as gossiping, spreading rumors, and making innuendoes. The intent is to damage the boss's image and standing in every way possible. A hunting party doesn't organize formally but instead seems just to emerge. It starts with a couple of very frustrated and angry people who begin gossiping about the boss and are then joined by more and more people. Hunting parties work more like a stone thrown into a pool of water with ever-widening ripples. Obviously there are no formal meetings—these are all casual conversations. There also is never a stated intent, but the intent is understood all the same. A hunting party has seductive power; it is easy to get drawn in by the excitement of being in an inner circle, of being in the know, and even of being engaged in the dangerous occupation of destroying the boss.

Now, here is the difficult piece for you. You signed on as a director to be a positive force engaged in positive actions. Even though the boss may deserve it, your engagement in any kind of negative, hostile action is really beneath you. There is something low about hunting parties because there is so much malice and underhandedness.

On the other hand, you do have to keep your ear to the ground. A hunting party is a significant event and as a director you have to know what is going on. So you have keep up and stay informed without becoming part of the inner circle and without engaging in spreading the rumors and gossip further.

Of course, one danger here is that people in any hunting party that would capture your attention are your peer group. You will be criticized, although rarely to your face, for not joining the inner circle—and your peers do know who is really in the party and who is just visiting. Here you might end up looking like you support the boss, that you let others do your dirty work, or that you don't like to get involved. You don't have to be a Switzerland. Instead, be steady and rational, keep doing what is right, be the voice of reason, and don't get swept up in the action. A hunting party often can get caught up in the thrill of the chase. The problem with any thrill is that it often clouds normally good judgment.

By the way, the boss usually gets wind of a hunting party, for there is always someone willing to tell the boss who is stirring up trouble, and will take action when the time is right against the inner circle. No boss wants that kind of direct threat to power and a nasty boss is likely to take nasty action. Other bosses are also watching and assessing for the future who is part of negative action in the organization.

One further thought. Always be aware of the agenda of the inner circle of a hunting party. Is it truly because each person wants to do right by the organization and get rid of a bad boss once and for all? Or do some individuals perhaps see an opportunity to create a vacancy in a position they have long desired? You might want to get rid of your bad boss but you don't want to be an unwitting stepping stone in someone else's career either. Be on alert when a hunting party forms.

Now, on to other issues. When dealing with a truly bad boss, it can be helpful to minimize in your own mind the boss's traits that are negative and focus instead on the better aspects of the boss's personality. Ask yourself continually if those negative traits are the whole story about your boss. We never really have a complete picture of anyone. Focusing away from the negative traits might help you to survive in this difficult situation.

It is always an impulse to stay as far away from a bad boss as possible. Certainly, one should keep their distance, but not too far, because out of sight is also out of mind when it comes to budget and other organizational resources.

In the end, if your boss is too abusive or engaged in illegal actions, you have no choice but to report the boss formally to the appropriate person such as the boss's boss or human resources. This is when it is a good time to be a part of a group if they are willing to step up too. To report or not report a boss is an exceptionally difficult dilemma. Formal reporting in some organizations will work out fine, as many will be relieved that a problem boss is finally getting the comeuppance so long deserved. Alas, in some organizations formal reporting can result in career suicide even if you are on the winning side both legally and morally because you then become known as a problem. After all, you took an action which exposed the organization's failings. As if that were not enough, your formal action might not have the result you intended and your boss gets to stay and you go. It is unfortunate that many people are forced to weigh their job against the chronic wrongdoing of a boss. That is why bad bosses get away with such abuses for so long. Our human instincts for survival are great, but fortunately, for the cause of justice, our courage is great too.

CONCLUSION

Every library director should know that it is imperative to have a good relationship with the boss. A happy boss makes life easier. An unhappy boss makes our work life very difficult. The message of this chapter is for you to become an expert on your boss by understanding the boss's needs, context, and work styles. Become a boss interpreter who will gauge accurately what the boss expects. This is your key to success with your boss.

————————————

For more writings by me on this subject, see "How to Spot a CIO in Trouble" with M. B. Ayati, *Educause Quarterly*, No. 4, 2003.

Chapter Three

Engaging Staff

Ninety-nine percent of us work because we have to. We have to put food on the table, make sure we have a roof over our heads, care for the young and the elderly, have medical care, and lead a decent, respectable, secure life. Most of us work hard throughout the day to retain our jobs and, if possible, get ahead to higher positions and higher salaries.

Work also provides a level of satisfaction and a sense of purpose. This is particularly true in libraries, where the mission is clearly beneficial to so many and to society overall. Staff can feel good about their work and about the service that they provide.

For a successful library, staff should be encouraged to be deeply engaged with their job and the mission of the library. A director should focus on inspiring staff to do their job to the fullest extent, to do it well, and to enjoy it. It isn't necessarily related to the time that a person puts in. Most staff will be 8 for 8: eight hours work for eight hours pay. Some will contribute countless hours to help the library achieve its goals. What matters most is when the staff is on the job that they are involved, attentive, and effective—in short, engaged. To achieve a culture of engagement, it is important for every director to know that the director's actions, behaviors, and attitudes impacts the staff's engagement with the library. Certain actions, behaviors, and attitudes can sustain the staff's engagement while others dispirit the staff and cause them to diminish their expectations of the library and their own contribution

The more engaged your staff is, the more you will have a library that is dynamic and vibrant. Every library director must continually build an internal environment that encourages staff to enjoy being in the library. In this chapter, we will take a look at those actions, behaviors, and attitudes that help staff to be engaged.

PEOPLE WHO LIKE PEOPLE

If ever there was a key to a successful library with an engaged staff, it is having a workplace where everyone really likes everyone and gets along well. It makes it a pleasure to come to work in the morning and to work side by side all day long with people whose company you like. An enjoyable workplace is a great motivator. People feel secure in this environment, creativity flows, and goals move forward.

When we are striving for this ideal workplace, we have to really like people ourselves. This doesn't mean that as directors we are giving out gifts and hitting the happy hour with staff. Instead we demonstrate one single and powerful characteristic: respect. Liking people is centered in respect. Respect means a real regard for the feelings and rights of others.

What happens if we don't have true respect for staff? When any of us disrespects another, resentment and anger builds. The person disrespected feels belittled and humiliated. Additionally, that person's friends take sides and line up in opposition. Every director should be careful that respect is always shown for people. The behavior of respect must be continually modeled.

Respect is shown in many ways. Listening well is a key element of respect. Naturally, every director should listen well anyway because the right information is critical for decision making. The quality of decision making is directly related to the quality of information received. But listening is also a profound symbol of respect. When you listen well, you say, "I have time for you" and "What you have to say is important to me." Take a moment and see how you listen. Are you really listening or just waiting until you have a chance to speak? Are you hearing the person's viewpoint, agenda, and concerns or thinking about your next meeting? Do you know what is really being asked or do you lose interest quickly? Are you interrupting or hurrying the person along? Are you jumping the gun by saying within a couple of minutes "Yes, I already know this situation and here is what I want you to do about this"? Are you multitasking while the person speaks such as checking your texts on your phone? All of this sends a clear message: you aren't important to me. If you demonstrate these behaviors often enough, good communication shuts down. Who wants to talk to someone who is never listening? You will soon be disrespected yourself.

I want also to stress that taking on a director's position does not entitle one to talk more. Sometimes people think that the higher they go in an organization, the more they have a right to talk while everyone else listens. Certainly facility with language is one of the keys to success for any director, but the staff are not there to sit at the feet of the master. We cannot hear what staff have to say or understand the issue if we are constantly talking.

Why do some directors talk so much? Part of it is a wish to dominate the environment, part of it is ego. The staff soon become very frustrated when they can't get a word in edgewise and are forced to listen to the director running on and on with more bombast than information. Instead, as directors, we should sit back and listen; we might just learn something we don't know.

Respect is also shown by knowing people's names. Certainly, some libraries have huge staffs and it is hard to know everyone. However, knowing who people are and what they do and where they work is a big element of respect. When you call people by name, it says "You are an individual to me and not just another cog in the wheel." When you first take on a director's position, work hard to learn people's names quickly. Meet everyone, and then reinforce your memory by getting out that organization chart, looking through the web directory, and putting faces to the names.

Respect also means never criticizing anyone publicly. This is commonly known, and yet we see it done. Sometimes people think that public criticism is an effective strategy because it shows the power and control of a director. In fact, it backfires horribly because the staff, even if they feel that the person deserves it, will still side emotionally with that individual. After all, they don't want to be next. If a director rules by fear, then staff soon learn not to put themselves in the way of any possibility of public humiliation. This means they won't take risks, and risk taking is vital for an organization to move forward. Criticism should always be done privately but also respectfully.

Instead, take public opportunities to support your people. Congratulate them on their successes. Laud their triumphs, and celebrate their achievements. This not only rewards the individual but also shows the group as a whole what can be achieved, what work is valued, and how good success is for all. It sets the bar high and encourages people to be engaged fully in their work.

Respect also means being sure to give credit where credit is due. There is nothing worse than a boss who takes the credit. Be fair; be gracious to the staff that got the project there even if your leadership set the stage. Let others shine through. The warmth of giving credit where it is due goes a long way in engaging people.

Respect is also shown by appreciating all levels of staff and all levels of contribution. You will have staff that are smarter, more talented, and more committed than others. There will be people who will make outstanding contributions. It is easy to appreciate and respect them. Just be sure to also respect the person who day in and day out does routine and often tedious work that nevertheless enables service to the customers.

Do be on time. Being late is a sign of disrespect. Sometimes it is easy when we get more powerful to forget that other people's time is valuable too. When you are late, the message is clear: My time is more valuable than yours. Yes, certainly a director's life is busy and lateness can occur, but when it does make sure that whoever is waiting for you knows what has happened and what your estimated time of arrival is. You don't want staff sitting there cooling their heels and getting annoyed. The mounting frustration of waiting on someone regularly will not help to build an engaged environment. I would also point out that if you are late often enough, your staff will begin to copy your behavior. Soon you will find that you are waiting for your staff to come to meetings.

Everywhere social commentators are deploring the deterioration of manners. All of us rush around checking our emails and our texts, worrying about our next meeting, concerned about the many deadlines next week and solving ten problems in our heads that we forget about the human dimension. Did we really just order a coffee and forget to say good morning? Did someone hold the door open for us and we sailed through without a nod of thanks? Our busy and stressful lives are conditioning us not to be fully present in our own lives. Be fully present in the moment and be aware of the people around you. Take time for people. Staff know you are busy but they will appreciate a nod, a wave, or a smile that shows that you see them as individuals that you care about.

I cannot stress enough the importance of being accessible to people as a sign of respect and liking for people. Certainly meetings, deadlines, decisions, and problems all crowd into the day. However, there must always be time for staff to speak with you. If staff cannot get an appointment until four weeks from now, they will often stop trying and you will miss critical information. Instead, send this message, "I do have busy days but if you need to speak to me, then we will always find some time." This isn't easy, but an inaccessible director sends a clear message that staff are not a priority.

I want also to note the importance of hiring people who like people, who have a capacity to relate to people, and who have a fundamental respect for others. People like this are pleasant to work with, are team players and nice colleagues, and are good at working with the customers. In fact, it helps to take the customer's point of view when hiring. Whom would the customers like to interact with? Many times in hiring, we say that this candidate meets the requirements, but we all know that possessing just the basic requirements is not what makes for an engaging employee. Yes, the skill set for the job has to be there but the personality is equally important. Hire the people-oriented candidate. Keep searching until you do find this right person for the job. Never compromise in hiring just because you can't find anyone for that job. If that continues, you will soon have a second-rate library. Better a vacancy than an unsuitable employee.

STAND-UP DIRECTOR

What does it mean to be a stand-up person? This is someone who can be trusted in any predicament, who can be counted on when things get tough, who will never abandon ship, and who will do what it takes for others no matter the difficulty.

A director has to be a stand-up director. Remember always that the director role is first and foremost a leadership role and being a stand-up person is an important part of leadership. Staff need to know that their leader will be there for them and for the library no matter what the challenges. If you buckle under challenges, staff will doubt your leadership and will disengage from you. So step up and never abdicate your role no matter how tough it gets.

Rod Hersberger: "Every director needs to understand that leadership is a shared experience. The director's task is to create and maintain a climate where good ideas are welcome and supported. As the best ideas rise to the top, the director becomes their advocate and champion. As the best ideas become successful programs, the director shares the credit and rewards as appropriate."

Certainly in times of crisis, a director has an opportunity to demonstrate the cool hand, the courage, the fearless commitment, and the reasoned judgment that will steer the library through the crisis. Fortunately, every day does not present crises such as earthquakes, tornadoes, or floods. Instead, think about the daily smaller ways that show that you are a stand-up director.

Let's look at examples of how you can show your support. When employees have a difficult situation, make sure you have their back. Here is a common one: a customer requests a meeting with you to complain about a staff member's behavior. Instead of judging the staff member on the spot, just take the information, tell the customer you will get back to him or her, and then speak with the staff member to hear thoroughly the other side of the story. More often than not the story will be quite different. Look for a solution together. This behavior on your part means that you support your staff.

Now sometimes a customer wants library policy to be bent and a staff member has rightly refused this. Because of political reasons, because the problem may not be worth the grief, or because you wish to be generous toward the customer, you are willing to make this accommodation for the customer. Make sure that you never decide this in a vacuum. Instead, talk over your reasoning with the staff member and see what the implications are. If you do decide to bend the policy, let the customer know that the staff member was correct and you are making a one-time accommodation. In short, your discussion with the customer should support your staff. Don't let the customer go back to the staff member with an attitude of "I win" or "gotcha." Also, consider letting the staff member follow up with the customer. The staff member can tell the customer that the "director has referred the concern back to me and I am willing to make this change one time." Certainly this might not fool the customer, since clearly you are the source of the action, but it does restore the staff member's control over the situation and helps the staff member to save face.

Customer service is a tough business, and we do get problem customers who range widely in inappropriate comments and behaviors with staff. Never let any customer disrespect your staff. Any customer whose speech or behavior is rude, outlandish, vulgar, racist, sexist, or otherwise offensive must know that such offenses will not be tolerated. A range of actions is available to you from talking with the offender, to banning the offender from the library for a period of time, or, if in the case of a university library, referring the student to the dean of students. As often as not, the staff member who was offended will ask you not to pursue any action since it is likely that the staff member dealt with the problem on the spot or does not wish to be involved more if it requires going to other units in the parent organization. You will have to judge whether the speech or behavior warrants more. But even if there is no further action, any staff member will really appreciate your willingness to stand up and address the problem.

Now sometimes staff can get themselves into trouble and do something really wrong. This can occur even with a good employee who has just misjudged the situation or didn't realize that he or she didn't have the experience to handle the situation. In such a case, you may be counseling or even disciplining the employee. But if you have an attitude of support, then your focus should be on correcting the behavior to get the employee into the right place and out of trouble. Then forgive and forget. Any staff member will deeply appreciate your support and attitude.

In this situation, be sure to look into what was motivating the employee. Look at the underlying issues with that employee. Obviously the employee needs more training, but sometimes there are reasons that a person oversteps the bounds. The reasons are many including having grown beyond the current job, being frustrated with the limitations of the position, not having enough challenges, or having an abundance of creativity with nowhere to take it. When dealing with a good staff member in trouble, it helps to look at the deeper reason. Once you understand that, you can solve the problem in the long term. Standing up doesn't just mean being courageous or supportive in the drama of the moment but also in providing continuing support that keeps the employee out of trouble in the future.

In terms of being a stand-up director, I want to stress the importance of never running down your own staff to others beyond the library. You must never criticize your staff to your boss, your board, your peers, or supporters. Not only will this hurt the image of the library, for which you are responsible, but it will also get back to the staff, and this will damage your supportive relationship with staff.

Of course never run down individuals in your staff to each other either. How can you claim to be supportive, to be there for people, if you are critical of them? Everyone knows that if you are critical of one person on your staff, then you can do this to them when their backs are turned. They will learn to be wary. Once mistrust starts, you will soon lose vital support.

Never permit anyone outside of the library to direct your staff inappropriately. If you are in a library that has a parent organization, sometimes people in other units, such as human resources or facilities management, will give your staff directives. Usually this is just normal business, as they might be clarifying policy or procedures or introducing a new minor process. People have to work across organizational lines in order for the work to flow properly. After all everything cannot go through you as there would be a massive logjam on your desk and you would be sunk in minutiae. However, once in a while, people in other units will cross the line into your territory and give inappropriate directives to your staff. Let's look at two examples.

Say that you are renovating the library and you discover that your project manager has been told by facilities management to make some changes in the plan without your approval. Or perhaps human resources has issued a negative decision to one of your employees on a pending reclassification without input from you or your managers. Such situations usually come to your attention from upset employees or upset middle managers in the library. Often, there is nothing malicious about these inappropriate directives however problematic. It usually stems from the staff member in the other unit overstepping boundaries, having a big ego, or not having the knowledge to understand the consequences. However, you cannot take this lying down.

This doesn't mean that you rush over with a full head of steam to confront that other unit's director even though some of these situations can make you very mad. Address the situation rationally as you would any other problem. Importantly, if it can be solved by another in the library then allow that. Save yourself for the big issues. But do address it. A courteous but clear message must be sent to the other unit that no one crosses into your territory and gives your staff inappropriate directives. Now, you might be concerned about having a conflict with this other unit. We will talk in an upcoming chapter about conflicts in the organization, but you shouldn't see it as a conflict. You are simply addressing a problem. Any reasonable fellow director would agree that staff in one unit cannot be receiving inappropriate directives from another unit. After all, how would that director like it if it happened to his or her own staff? Now, one caution, if the issue is big enough, let your boss know, since this situation might get back to your boss but with a spin that does not put you in a favorable light.

Don't be concerned that you are going to get a reputation because of your willingness to fight for your territory. This is not a bad thing—other units should know that you can't be messed with. They will think twice before taking you on.

Now the staff that was affected by these inappropriate directives will deeply appreciate that you stood up for them and for the library. They will like that you could not be pushed around and would not let them be pushed around either. So will the rest of the staff in the library, because this type of event will be the gossip of the week. This is good PR for you with your staff and helps you to build your image as a stand-up director.

Going on to other issues, be mindful always to keep your promises or be prepared to explain why you didn't. Staff have to be able to rely on you. If not, they will soon disengage from you. Of course, be very careful never to promise what you cannot deliver.

Along this line, never promise an employee a job. It is sometimes tempting to promise an upcoming job to a very good employee, especially if you think this person is getting on the market for another position. When this promise goes wrong, and it often does, there are not only serious legal issues ahead but also serious morale issues. You will have both an angry employee confronting you with your broken promise and angry applicants confronting you because you have not played fair. By the way, don't think you can keep a job promise a secret. An employee who has been promised a job by the director will likely talk about it, since it not only boosts his or her pride and standing but also warns off other applicants.

Do be there for people when they are ill or when a tragedy strikes. So many sad things can happen and the director needs to be there for people. Some directors act as if death or serious illness is just a terrible inconvenience for the library. This callousness will be remembered. Staff will rightly judge such a director as heartless.

Don't ask people to do what you wouldn't do yourself. Sometimes being directors goes to our heads and we take ourselves and our positions too seriously. If you are asking people to do things, then be sure you can, will, or would do it yourself. Remember that you can show this right attitude in many small daily actions. It doesn't have to be just the big things. For example, do you have a meeting that has to be set up at the last minute? You can move tables too. Pitching in doesn't rob you of your dignity but instead sends a clear statement that you are not above it all.

Always be values driven. If a director is driven by values, it means that there is an unshakable core upon which the staff can rely. Let me give an example. Say that you have been unreachable for whatever reason and the staff has to make a sudden significant decision in your absence. When you are back in touch and the staff says to you, "we knew this is what you would want us to do" then you know that your values have been transmitted. Staff took the risk of a decision because they knew what the values that you stood upon were.

On this point also, make sure that the staff is not afraid to take action. Sometimes directors can get angry when staff has taken the wrong action that has to be cleaned up. If staff have taken action that they genuinely thought was right but turned out to be wrong, just view it as a learning experience for the staff. Clean up the problem with them. It is easy to make a mistake, particularly in an emergency situation, but it is better that the staff tried to solve the problem. After all, you don't want to have a staff that is risk averse. How engaged will they be if they are scared to take action?

Being a stand-up director also means building a culture of generosity in the library. Standing up for people means that we are generous to them, that we give them the benefit of the doubt, that we get the facts before judging, that we have the spirit of forgiveness, that we are willing to forget, that we have tolerance and understanding for the foibles of humans, and that we know that we never know the full story about any other person. A director committed to engaging people should always model generous behavior. Don't look for public thanks for being generous but know that you are building a good organization.

NOT ONE OF THE GANG

It may seem contradictory, but becoming friends with your staff is not a way to engage staff. Be friendly but not a friend. You are the director and not one of the gang. Don't cross the line by trying to be friends with your staff, and don't permit staff to try and be friends with you either. I know it is harsh but look at it this way.

You cannot make clear judgments and decisions about people when you are their buddy. As a director, your role is to support the good of the entire library, not individuals. When the interests of individuals and the library coincide, it is a happy moment but, if they don't, then your responsibility always lies with the welfare of the whole library. If you are a good friend to several members of the staff, they will expect you to act as a friend and make favorable decisions for them concerning performance evaluations, raises, assignments, transfers, and other important benefits. If favorable decisions are not possible for whatever reasons, and you act as a boss and not as a friend, disappointment and resentment will take hold. And there is no enemy like a former friend.

This is particularly tough for those of you who grew up in a library and rose to the director position. You made a lot of friends during this time. They probably celebrated your rise, with only a little jealousy, and now feel comfortable that you are in charge. How do you handle decisions affecting your friends? Just be scrupulously fair to all and transparent about decisions. However, do be prepared for some of those friendships to fall off or change. The common bonds that held you together with your friends are now breaking with your increased power, your new perspective on organizational issues, and the time you are spending with new groups as a result of being a director. Many friendships will survive but many will never be the same again.

Do be careful about conversations with staff. Sometimes staff will tell a director incredibly personal things that do not have a bearing on the workplace. Where you can, head these conversations off at the pass, but if you can't, don't engage in them or follow up later by asking questions about what happened. It doesn't mean you have to be cold, but don't be familiar either. You are not one of the gang with whom staff should be sharing private information. Staff will often come to regret that they shared this information and will resent you having this knowledge about them. Because of embarrassment, they may even avoid you for some time.

One of the strangest experiences you may have as a director is when a spouse or significant other of one of your staff asks to speak with you and tells you about any range of issues including pending separations and child custody battles. Rarely is there is a good and pure motivation behind this: usually, it is malicious in intent. All you can do is listen respectfully but then show the person out the door as soon as possible. You do need to inform the staff member of what happened—obviously the response will be both anger and embarrassment. Keep out of it and don't change any of your behavior toward the employee. One caveat, if the spouse or significant other has told you that your staff member has a substance abuse or gambling problem, talk with that person's supervisor and keep an eye on the situation for any indications that these claims are true. Such problems will enter the workplace sooner or later.

At the same time, keep your own personal life personal. You are not one of the gang who can easily chat about personal business. As a director, you will be talked about, and the more information you put out there, the more people will talk. Just remember that you are news. The state of your marriage, problems with kids, and financial challenges are all private matters and must remain so. Your job is to be interested in others not to be endlessly talking about yourself. Your problems may raise sympathy here and there, but too much familiarity encourages people to take liberties, which eventually erodes your power as a director.

Be careful never to have favorites. Certainly there will be people that you will like more. That is only natural. There is chemistry between people. However, chemistry cannot cloud your judgment. People are quick to spot if the director has favorites. Sometimes these are imagined, but it is a serious problem because it calls into question your fairness. Be careful particularly about the jealousy between units in the library. In particular, staff will be quick to assume that the administrative unit gets all the benefits even if it isn't true. Just be very transparent about who gets what equipment, what resources, and what staff.

If you are a person who is good at mentoring, do protect your mentee's status. Be clear through your fair actions and fair decisions that the person is a mentee and not a favorite. Staff groups can be harsh on the "blue-eyed boy or girl" who has a bigger share of the director's time. Don't let it discourage you from mentoring though, as it is a good policy to develop talented staff.

Do be mindful about who gets your ear. Everybody has an agenda for you. Now you may have a staff member who is really tops and particularly worthy of having your ear. Just never be exclusive because this will turn off the others and again they will stop communicating.

One thing that will always distinguish a director is the many ceremonial duties. You speak at all library staff meetings, you welcome visitors, and you are the master of ceremonies at dedications and events. The leadership position requires you to be continually out front. Sometimes, this can be exhausting and it is tempting to slide back to be one of the gang. But you are not. People need to see their leader, to hear what you have to say. This doesn't mean that you don't give others a shot at these opportunities—speaking in public at a variety of events is a good training ground—but you cannot abdicate this role either. Make sure that you are where you need to be, speaking about what is important. If you are not there, your message is clear—you aren't engaged or concerned.

THE FIGHTER IN THE RING

There is nothing tougher than a serious employee problem. These problems can run the gamut. There can be mental illness, harassment, continual conflicts, open hostility, illegal behavior, threatening comments and attitudes, a failure of duties, continued unexplained absences, substance abuse, and on and on. It would be a rare, and very lucky, director who does not encounter one of more of these issues in a career.

The presence of these individuals is very demoralizing and sometimes frightening to the staff. If you want people to be engaged in the workplace, there must be harmony. People will rightly look to you to solve the problem and restore the harmonious environment.

Therefore, you must deal with problems and be unafraid of conflict. You are the one who must have the tough conversations, who must make the difficult decisions, and who has to take the disciplinary action. Naturally you don't go this alone—your human resources department and your boss must be behind you to make sure that you are completely within your rights and completely on target with your process. Be careful to comply with their directives, as that provides you with a level of legal protection.

When you take on a problem employee, that person is going to strike back hard at you. You have become the target. You have to be a fighter in the ring. You are going to punch and get punched back. However, this is not a power struggle although the problem employee will want to see it that way. Remember you are the one with the power. You are the heavyweight. Keep this in mind even if you want to quake in your boots when facing down a serious problem employee.

> ***Connie Vinita Dowell***: "Hiring along with retaining, supporting, and promoting the best staff may be the most important thing you can do. Review openings carefully making every position count. Make recruiting and hiring a priority. Enlist external colleagues and make a community goal of hiring and choosing the best. Don't give up on the best candidate easily if they say no. Support your best staff with thank yous, bonuses, equity adjustments, and more to reward outstanding people. Celebrate shared and individual success at every opportunity. Fund professional development to develop skills and promote the best staff."

The thought of getting punched, which can take many forms— malicious gossip, overly hostile behavior toward you, whistleblowing even when there is nothing to whistleblow about, filing of grievances, and even lawsuits—is enough to frighten anyone, but that is why you have the position. It is your job to clean up problems even if the cost is high.

Think about it this way, if you don't clean up the problem, then who is in charge? Yes, it is the problem employee. And remember that performance standards are set by the lowest performing member of the group. If you don't clean up the problem, you have permitted your standards to be lowered to the level of the problem employee. Is this the type of library that you want?

Sometimes it is tempting to dodge these problems. Say for example that the problem employee is a few levels below you in the organization. Obviously, the supervisor, under your overall guidance, has many actions to take to manage this employee. However, this does not mean that you dump everything on the supervisor. You must stand by the supervisor and be prepared to do your part.

You also are dodging the problem if you reduce an incompetent employee's duties in order to minimize the damage to the work that the employee can do. This is called a workaround and the meaning of workaround is to circumvent a problem but not eliminate it. You and your supervisors might be saying to yourselves that you have found a solution to the problem. Your staff, who are watching closely, are saying that you have appeased a problem employee who is making the same salary as before but with fewer duties. Human resources is saying that you have lost your capacity to track the employee's performance at the level that the job requires because you reduced the employee's duties. This means that you likely never will be able to dismiss the incompetent employee. Don't kid yourself with a workaround. You know you are dodging the problem. Do you really need employees that don't make a contribution? Additionally, workarounds don't solve the problem because problem employees are a problem wherever they are and whatever they are doing.

Here is another example. Sometimes when a problem employee doesn't get along with others, is hostile, or even creepy, it is tempting to move the employee's workstation into an isolated location so that he or she interacts less with other staff. The staff often like this because for them the problem is out of sight and out of mind. The problem employee usually likes it too since then he or she is away from the watchful eye of the supervisor. However, if the supervisor cannot see the employee's behavior all the time, then again the supervisor cannot track the employee's performance, and without tracking there is no hope of dismissal. Make the employee do the job where and how it is supposed to be done or face dismissal.

If the problem employee is a high-level manager, it can be tempting to try and get along with this manager at all costs in order to avoid a shoot-out in the executive suite. But a high-level manager, who wields a lot of power, has the capacity to do a lot of damage. You will give the manager a chance to change, of course, but if you don't see change in the way you want it and on the schedule you want, fire the problem manager quickly before more damage is done. The staff will thank you for it.

It is also tempting to have harmony at all costs. While we strive for harmony in the workplace, not everything is a kumbaya moment. You can't engage people if they see you dodging the tough problems and not working through the difficult situations in a false attempt to create harmony in the workplace. While you don't want to become a facilitator for every problem, even though people will look to you to do so, you also cannot ask them just to get along when there is a serious problem employee in their midst. If there is a minor problem, certainly people should be grown-ups and solve their own conflicts but with serious matters, it is your responsibility.

I do want to note that sometimes supervision can make us hard because so frequently it is the problems that land on our desks: the conflicts, the difficult person, the employee in trouble. We don't always see the best of human behavior. As difficult as this is sometimes, don't let the difficulties with problem staff color your outlook about people. In other words, don't let it get to you. It is like watching the news every night. If the news, full of murder, hostility, and distress, is all that we ever knew about human beings, we would have a very sorry picture of humankind. Fortunately, we know that most people in this world are good and trying to do the right things by family, friends, and society.

THE ACTOR ON THE STAGE

There is nothing worse than a grumpy director. Grumpiness can take many forms. It could be a director who isn't a morning person, shouldn't be talked to before the first cup of coffee, looks irritated when a problem is mentioned, is annoyed when someone calls in sick, and so on. Here is what I would say. When you became the director, you became an actor on the stage. Your role requires you to be positive and outgoing. Certainly there will be days when you might not feel this way, but get a grip. You must continually role model the behavior you expect in the library. Don't say "good morning"? Soon others won't either. Don't say "good night" or "hello, how are you"? Others soon won't either. Do you really want a place full of indifferent and grumpy behavior?

A director's position is not an indulgent one. Any actor will be fired if they don't play the part. You are an actor too for this role. Being positive is contagious in the workplace. Think about the kind of workplace that you want.

You might say that you have the right to be yourself. Yes, so then be the best of you. Grumpy, irritated behavior is selfish. Who gave you the right to pollute the workplace with a grumpy attitude? And you will only have yourself to blame if the rest of the staff follows.

CHECKING YOUR EGO

Obviously, directors have a healthy ego, otherwise they would not be there. But ego is something that must always be held in check. If we want to engage staff fully, we cannot turn them off by displaying a needy or giant ego. Think about these things.

Don't be afraid to say, "I made a mistake." If you made a mistake, and every director does, so you made a mistake. You can't let your ego get in the way of the work. The question is what is the right decision now for the library? You might not have had enough information before when you made the wrong decision or you were just off your game. It doesn't matter, just admit it and move forward. Never be afraid of reversing a decision.

Likewise, don't be afraid to say, "I'm sorry." Sometimes as directors, we really goof. We may have completely misread a situation for many reasons—chief among which is being overworked and overly tired. If you really hurt people's feelings, then apologize. If you don't, it will fester for the individual who is harmed. Do you want to be a big person or a small one?

Sometimes as directors we think that we have to know it all. We think that if we show that we don't know every detail about every service in the library, then the staff will think less of us. Remember what I said in the first chapter that we are now masters of integration of the systems of the library. You can't stay up with the detail about every service and still have time to focus on being a good director. If you don't know something about a service, say so and ask the staff questions about it. Never pretend to know what you don't. First of all, your ignorance will show in no time, which makes you look silly, and second, you will hurt your decision making if you don't get the facts from the staff. Consult, consult, consult, because your ego in the way can steer you wrong. Besides, the staff will love having the chance to show you their expertise.

As part of this, we also have to be careful not to be a know-it-all. It is easy for us to assume once we reach the position of a director that therefore we know more than others. While any director has a unique and special view born of experience and responsibility, we also must be very aware of the knowledge and skills of others.

Be mindful of the power of power and don't let it go to your head. Feeling powerful is very seductive to any ego—it makes us feel important, even invincible. Once power takes hold of our ego then it is easy to start abusing it. Now, you might be saying to yourself, "what power?" However, a director controls all resources, positions, facilities, goods, and so on. There actually is a great deal of power. A director can give out prized assignments, a better work schedule, a nicer office, better furniture, more funds for travel, merit pay, promotions, or the latest technology as examples. How do we abuse this power? Mostly it is when we reward and punish through the allocation of these tangible and intangible goods.

Now, let me deliberately send you a mixed message. On the one hand, you don't want to turn into a mafia boss who sees staff as either with you or against you and who only allocates goods to those who are squarely in your camp. On the other hand, you are not going to give a problem or marginal employee a nice work schedule or the only office with a window. Nor are you going to give an employee who takes every opportunity to oppose you a plum assignment. While you don't want to abuse power, you also don't want to be a fool. You are not to be walked over. You must command respect. What you will do is give people what they need to do their job and never withhold resources or goods that will make a difference in the successful completion of assignments. Anything less would be against the best interests of the library.

Consider that when we abuse power, we do lose it. Let's go back to the mafia boss as an example. A mafia boss creates camps or divisions in the staff. This inevitably turns into infighting and other pathological behaviors that will damage the culture of the library over time. Also, the staff will resent and be hostile covertly toward any mafia boss for abusing power. The unrest in the library will come to the attention of the director's boss and the director shortly will be saying goodbye to the job. The damaged culture, the infighting, and the hostility—all the result of the director's actions—are simply too nasty for any boss to tolerate for long.

Finally, check your ego and don't take anything personally. Sometimes it may feel very personal indeed if you are criticized or gossiped about, but remember this is just organizational life. If you take things too personally all the time, you will spend a fair part of your career depressed. Ask yourself, who is in charge here? Are you going to react to whatever is said about you or be in control of your reactions? When you take things too personally, you become a victim rather than a manager. Remember that to manage means to control successfully. Understand that some things just go with the territory. Instead, continually think about what is best for the library and keep moving on.

THE POWER SEEKERS

Any person in a leadership position must closely observe the flow of power around an organization. We just discussed the power that a director has and how carefully it has to be used. However, we are not the only ones who are holding power. Power can also be held by other people such as other managers, especially those in operations, finance, and technology; by staff who are experts; by staff who have high degrees of likability; and by staff who are known as "go to" people for those who need help. This range of power is only natural and is vital for moving the library's goals and operations forward.

Sometimes there are individuals who are seeking power for their own gain rather than for the welfare of the whole. There can be a lot of reasons for people to seek power: hostility toward you, the need to control, undue eagerness for advancement, and a large ego. You might begin to detect them in this way: they speak at meetings in a way that sounds as if they are rallying the troops, they are a major provider of gossip, they spend an undue amount of time lunching and socializing, they attempt to form cartels that may become a voting bloc on important issues, they hold premeetings with people of like minds in order to organize a stand before everyone else's voices can be heard. Power seekers can cause a lot of trouble in a library because they upset the rational process of decision making by continually advancing their own agenda.

As an alpha that has to lead, you cannot have a shadow organization. While there is little overt action you can take, keep a close watch on this situation because one day they might come for you. Be careful not to give power seekers any more organizational power than they may already have: keep them off powerful committees, reduce their visibility in library events, give their followers some interesting projects so they can begin to break away from the power seekers' grip, and step up your own interaction with the followers so that their loyalties will be divided. In short, you need to reengage this staff in your direction. Does this all sound Machiavellian? Yes, but you have a library at stake and you cannot permit power seekers to disrupt it.

BUILDING THE MANAGEMENT TEAM

A good management team—a core of trusted advisors—is critical for the success of any director committed to having an engaged staff. Managers who have weaknesses in ability or personality or who can't get along with each other bleed off important time and energy from you and from your staff. Even one weak manager can debilitate the staff and cause them to disengage. Make every effort to build the finest management team that you can, and if you have one already, appreciate it deeply. What makes a good member of a management team? Here are the characteristics: professional, dedicated, values-driven, imaginative, kind of heart, positive in attitude, helpful, alert to issues and problems, politically aware, courageous, interested in all things that concern the library, enjoying the achievements of others, confident in dissent but loyal to the final decision, confidential, clear eyed with unbiased opinions rooted in knowledge and fact, and free of agenda except for the welfare of the library.

Happy the staff (and happy the director) who has this kind of management team at the top—highly capable and continually cooperating for the success of all.

DRIVING THE STAFF CRAZY

There are certain behaviors on the part of directors that simply drive the staff crazy. Here are some: complaining about your workload to them even though you make more money, not responding to reports submitted or leaving emails unanswered, always missing deadlines including your own, being annoyed if staff have to call you on weekends or evenings, being totally out of touch on vacation, vacillating in decision making, demanding work at the last minute because of your lack of planning, delegating parts of the job that clearly belong to you, being ill-prepared for meetings, being inflexible or uneven in applying policies, failing to be gracious in greeting and thanking staff, losing your temper, being an elitist and acting entitled, and chronically coming in late to work.

While this seems like an incredible list, we have all witnessed directors who have some of these characteristics. It does drive the staff crazy because it impedes the work. Eventually staff get very frustrated in working with such a director and begin to disengage.

It is important for us all to remember that we are continually modeling behavior for those who work for us. You set the standards. The library will be filled with the behaviors listed above if you indulge in those behaviors.

If you are not yet convinced of the importance of changing this behavior, then look at it this way. While having one or two of these bad behaviors might not be enough to bring a director down, having several will put you at considerable risk. Your fall won't happen right away but the gradual loss of your credibility, the erosion of respect from the staff, and the continual gossip about your weaknesses will eventually reach the ear of your boss or your board. If you see yourself anywhere on this list, correct these behaviors now before it costs you your job.

MINDING THE MESSAGE

Information is the business of libraries, and everyone who works in libraries has quite a craving for information. If you want an engaged staff, do feed this craving by letting them know what is going on. They like to feel involved. They like to hear the information first.

Regular communication from the director is vital. Emails, newsletters, internal blogs, town halls, and so on are all ways in which we can communicate regularly. Keep a running list of things that happen that would be good for the staff to know. It is surprising what you forget after a busy week. Staff achievements, awards, publications, goals met, budgets, and so on are all vital. Make your communication regular, fun, positive, and informal. This is you talking to the staff even if you are fortunate enough to have a staff person who writes for you.

Scott Walter: "The one thing that every library director should know is that what matters most are the people. When you prepare to be a director, you may be thinking about trends in technology, challenges in publishing, or the needs of facilities, budgets, assessment, and so on, but, in the end, the success of your library and your success as its director all depend upon your commitment to its people."

Regular communication from the director is excellent internal public relations. Seeing achievements of fellow staff, for example, gives the staff a sense of pride in the library. It also helps them to get to know each other—which is a particular challenge in a large library with college or branch libraries or any system that is far flung. If people know each other even a little better, they are much more comfortable and engaged in the workplace.

I do know that regular communication takes time and sometimes it is hard to find the time. However, one of the main criticisms hurled by the staff at any director is "we never know what is going on." If you do hear that criticism, ask the staff, what it is that they don't know. Ask them for specifics. If you hear specifics, then you know you have work to do. If you don't, then you have just challenged an assumption about yourself and have laid some of it to rest. Of course, this is a complaint that never ends.

Regular communication is worth every effort because the staff feel much more engaged when they are in the know.

STAFF MORALE

Perhaps you have been doing all that you can and yet someone says to you that staff morale is bad. There is almost no statement more disheartening to a conscientious director than hearing about bad morale. Before you react, do consider the source. Is that person habitually negative? Is it a person that is covertly hostile toward you and knows exactly where to stab? Remember that one person cannot speak for the entire staff even though the person thinks that he or she is speaking for all. On the other hand, it might be that this is the one fearless person who tells you the truth about staff morale. One sure clue is that if you hear about bad morale from more than one person, then you might indeed have a problem.

If that is the case, then consider an employee assessment to get input on how staff see you, their jobs, the library, and staff morale. Ask the staff to be specific in their comments and suggestions for improvement. The input that you receive likely will be along a broad spectrum from the most negative (there is always the poison pen) to the most positive. However, if the input is largely negative and from a sizable portion of the staff, then it is time to address the issue of staff morale. Look closely at the staff's concerns and suggestions and develop and implement a plan of action.

You might be very upset about the input when you thought you were doing so well, but deal with staff morale as you would any other workplace issue. We already talked about not taking things personally, but learning about declining staff morale always hits a director particularly hard. Avoid apologizing to everyone as you work out your anxiety over a negative review. Forget about that hangdog expression and hold your head up high while you tackle the problem in a thoughtful and concentrated manner.

Simultaneously consider these actions: keep staff aware of the importance of their job and what the library means to the customer, take time to celebrate achievements and accomplishments, make sure that the work stations of the staff are comfortable, have fun with staff from time to time with events that are not work related, give staff important projects that they are passionate about, consider cross-training to let staff try something new, reduce the paperwork and bureaucracy where you can, and shake up the routine from time to time. Remember that employees make or break a business, so you want to attend to employee morale issues continually.

Penny Markey: "Every director should create an atmosphere in his or her library so that all staff members celebrate children, teens, and families. The director should provide youth services staff with support and adequate resources. Mentor them. Provide your youth librarians with guidance but at the same time give them opportunities to grow and be creative. Provide training and expect your youth services librarians to be good managers; also provide the opportunities for them to be excellent representatives of the library as they reach out into the community."

RELATIONSHIPS IN THE WORKPLACE

Some days you may feel that you are living in a soap opera. Libraries do have a strong element of the soap about them—staff searching for a mate, falling in love, breaking up, and getting married. Add to this that many of a library's part-time workers are young people whose quest for a partner occupies a sizable part of their brain. Most of these situations we simply observe because, apart from the occasional drama, it is all just part and parcel of life's great cycles. But sometimes these cycles do impact the workplace and become the domain of the director's work.

But before we look at a few situations, I just want to say this: regarding yourself and any romantic attraction you might have to someone on your staff, don't you dare! More often than not, this leads to disastrous and unpredictable consequences.

Now, moving on, it is not uncommon for an employee to come to see a director to explain about a serious matter of the heart that might be impacting his or her performance. It is a rare person who has a major life-changing event that doesn't spill into the workplace. Usually this is a very conscientious employee who has the awareness to make a preemptive strike by sharing personal information before you notice the slippage in performance. This knowledge is helpful to you because it will enable you to cut the employee some slack for a while. This is what the employee is hoping for as opposed to getting into trouble with a deteriorating performance.

However, as we discussed before, be careful not to be drawn into the conversation more than is necessary. Your heart might go out to the employee and you might respond emotionally to the employee's need to talk to relieve anxiety and pain, but under no circumstances give advice —you are the boss not a lawyer or therapist.

It does seem to me that the once forbidden territory of relationships between coworkers has loosened and there is now more dating and marriage or partnerships between coworkers. Unfortunately, this also means that there are break-ups and divorces. If both parties still work in the library when a break-up or divorce occurs, be very mindful not to take sides even if they each attempt to get you on one side or the other and even if you do think that one has been a jerk. Remember they may reconcile to each other but not to you since you took sides.

If one partner gets into trouble in the workplace and is undergoing disciplinary action sometimes the other partner will attempt to intrude into the process by various means including seeking a meeting with you, trying to attend the counseling/disciplinary hearing, or sending you emails defending the partner. Obviously you cannot permit this, as your business is with the one in trouble not with the partner. Everyone can understand the emotional bond that partners have and the need to defend each other, but still you have to draw the line—a personnel action is a confidential action. The employee may share what is happening, but you may never involve anyone who is outside the formal process no matter what the relationship. Make this clear, otherwise shortly both partners will be in trouble with you.

Physical and emotional attractions can take an unsettling or very nasty turn including behavior that is unseemly, troubled, unwanted, disturbed, illegal, or dangerous. Here are examples: an angry partner of an employee who enters the workplace to fight with the employee; staff who receive threatening messages from former partners; staff who are being stalked; any attachment between a supervisor and employee because of the possibility or even the appearance of sexual harassment; inappropriate physical behavior in the workplace regardless of consent or relationship; and one-sided, uncomfortable, unwanted, and sometimes dangerous attraction.

You already know to get on these issues fast even though such problems are very complicated. Of course, none of these should you manage alone. You must always work under the guidance of the human relations department, your boss, and possibly the police and legal department. Not only do such people provide you with essential expertise but also their guidance protects you if the situation goes south, which it easily can, especially when you are dealing with the darkest sides of human behavior. Additionally, if you don't get on the problem fast, the rest of your staff, depending upon the situation, can have a range of reactions from being deeply frightened, to wanting to stay away from work, to being disgusted, to being sick and tired of it, to eventually being angry at you for not solving it—emotions that are hardly conducive to an engaged staff focused on quality service. There are also serious legal implications for you personally for not managing an uncomfortable, dangerous, or illegal situation.

UNION ACTIONS

A library director can have a wide variety of roles relating to unions. Directors in unionized environments have the responsibility of making sure that the library's policies, processes, and actions are in compliance with the union contracts. Additionally, we handle union representatives in the workplace, requests for space for union meetings, and so forth. Such things are routine and controlled by explicit policies and procedures. But there are two areas that deserve particular attention—one is grievances and the other is when contract negotiations are underway.

Let me talk for a moment about grievances. Generally speaking, there is no reason for you to encounter more than a handful of grievances throughout your career. Why? Because you are going to keep your ear to the ground and make sure your supervisors have their ears to the ground too. You are going to be told about problems early and you are going to get on these problems and work out issues informally. Sometimes grievances are filed because the problem has lingered too long, and the employee has not been heard. I know it is harsh to hear this, but there can be a failure in management when a grievance is filed. While you are solving the grievance, do think about what could have been done differently to forestall this action. Naturally, you will get grievances, but too many should tell you, and it certainly will tell your boss, that you have a problem.

Having said that, by no means is it always your fault or the fault of your managers. You could have a crazy staff member who files continually. The good news is that this employee is not only annoying you but also the union representatives and human resources. In this case, do speak with human resources and see if they can work out something with the union representative. Some union representatives are willing to have a talk with the employee because silly grievances do not serve the purpose of the union.

You may also be a new director and have inherited a library whose staff has a culture of filing grievances. This will take a while to turn around, but gradually staff will come to realize with your open, committed, engaged, and problem-solving style, that grievances are the last resort not the first.

It could also be that the union wants to grieve over a policy of the parent organization and it just so happens that there is an opportunity to have a library employee file the grievance. Obviously, you can't solve this grievance so you just have to follow the procedures and pass it up to the next level.

Here is the point. In every grievance, keep your eye on the ball—which is to continually build a positive and enjoyable environment within the library. While you might be very upset by the grievance and you certainly won't be pleased at the amount of time it takes, maintain every courtesy toward the employee, the union representative, and their legal counsel. The latter two might give you the cold shoulder because that is part of the game, but you have a bigger game to play—the success of your library. If you pass the employee in the hall or you are awkwardly the only two riding up in the elevator, be your usual professional and courteous self. Remember you want this employee back on the team, and you can't get the person back if you demonstrate a hostile manner.

One footnote: sometimes an employee will say, "I am going to file a grievance." This is usually an attempt to intimidate you. Employees think that managers are frightened by grievances. But if you are sure you are on the right course and doing the right things, let this comment be water off a duck's back. In fact, when you hear this comment, mentally respond, "Then file." Be careful you don't accidentally say that out loud though!

Next, one of the most serious challenges for any director comes when contract negotiations are underway. Some directors may participate as management on bargaining teams, some may be the decider in contract negotiations and some might simply be observers while the union deals with the parent organization. When contract negotiations turn sour, there can be some ugly consequences such as work stoppages and strikes. Such union actions can divide the staff from the director. Here are some tips on being in this situation.

No matter how bad the situation gets, you must always be mindful of your own behavior. If you are the decider in contract negotiations, you might have staff very angry at you with ugly words said and printed. You might find pictures of yourself on posters or in ads in newspapers. You might have a picket line outside your library. Just keep in mind that while you must manage the immediate crisis, your focus should be on when the crisis is resolved because you have to have the staff return to a level of normalcy. Never forget that union actions are usually brief but the life of the library is very long.

Don't take any gamesmanship personally. Both sides will be doing whatever they can to get what they want. As personal as it may get sometimes, view it for what it is and don't let the rhetoric get to you.

Speaking of gamesmanship, do watch out for elected officials or wannabes who might use the turmoil about the library as an opportunity to gain not only some press headlines but also the support of labor which has some big dollars for future campaigns. Hopefully, you have reached out before the union actions started to any relevant elected official with the background information so that the management side is clear. Sometimes this information doesn't matter anyway, since that elected official has another purpose.

Heavy union action will put everyone in the library and yourself into turmoil so it will consume much of your thinking. It is only natural that you will want to talk about it and comment on all that is happening. It might even be that you sympathize with staff—this occurs sometimes when you yourself are just part of a large parent organization. You might agree that the staff needs a pay raise or better medical benefits as examples. No matter what your situation is, keep your thoughts and your sympathies to yourself. Make no comments publicly or privately unless you are required to do so for organizational purposes—such as a press release stating the management position. If you have a parent organization, be guided by the parent organization as to your role. Just remember that one misplaced comment from you, however informal, could be used against you, could advantage the union against your parent organization, and could earn you the anger of your boss. If your comments are damaging enough, you could actually get dismissed. Remember that in union action the lines are drawn and you are management.

Now, not all staff will agree with the union actions and may complain to you. It is only natural, because they are used to talking issues over with you. In this case, you neither agree nor disagree. Instead, refer them to their union.

Now if your staff goes on strike and there is a picket line in front of the library, you do have to cross it to get to work. Being at work will be required of you as management. Also, likely you and other managers are trying to keep library service going or at least keep the doors open. Crossing a picket line is a terribly awkward situation. Do it with as much grace and courtesy and politeness as you can muster. Don't engage in dialog, no matter what questions are hurled at you, but keep moving. If you have had a good relationship with your staff all along, they also are not interested in having a confrontation with you. Even though some staff might be caught up in the excitement, most will have no desire to make an enemy of you. However, your staff might not be the only ones on the picket line. If things get ugly, back away. Do consider that you and the other managers should get to work very early and go in the back door if you have one. On the one hand, you want to avoid looking like you are skulking about; on the other hand, you want to avoid confrontation. And, no, obviously you can't call in sick, as this action would rightly be judged by your fellow managers and your boss as cowardly. The worst part is that you actually might be sick but drag yourself to work anyway. You also might have had travel plans; cancel them if you can because again you will look cowardly. Few will believe that you really had travel plans even if you send a photo of yourself with your boarding pass pinned to your jacket.

As hard as some of this can be, it is even harder when the staff come back to work. Staff will still be angry and upset over the turmoil of the situation and sometimes embarrassed over their own behavior. Some will come in to see you later and tell you they had no choice—some just don't have the courage of their convictions and now don't want to pay the price of docked wages and docked benefits. However, one can never underestimate peer pressure; some people really don't want to be engaged in a strike but the pressure to be with the group, and the fear of being shunned for not participating, was simply too great. Staff are also under heavy pressure by union leadership—after all, the business of the union is to perpetuate itself. How effective would the union be if staff did not comply with strikes or other work actions?

Strikes don't always bring out the best in people. When staff return to work, be careful to treat them exactly the same as before even if they have been among the most vicious. Your focus has to be on healing. However, some people are so nasty in these situations that it may be years before you get that image completely out of your head.

You will find that staff may be harder on each other at this time. Heavy union actions can tear people apart. They have argued with each other about negotiations; they are accusing each other over docked wages; they feel frustrated with each other if the negotiations did not go their way. The worst of course is very hard feelings toward staff who crossed the picket line. Sometimes it takes years for people to forgive each other for this. In all honesty, there is not much you can do. This is not your fight. Just get back to business as soon as possible but do cut people some slack in the immediate aftermath, as they will be tired and upset.

> *Peter Hepburn*: "At the start of my career I thought that I needed to respond immediately and thoroughly to all communications, especially email. I've learned that taking time to give a response proper consideration is often more effective and that my replies can be short and to the point."

THE POLITICALLY CONNECTED STAFF

There are two types of politically connected staff. One is the staff who is a good friend, relative, or ally of an elected official. The other is the person who is a good friend, relative, or ally of someone at a higher rung in the organization. Engaging these individuals is fraught with problems.

The problem doesn't come when the employee uses the connections for good. Although that can be a small problem since that employee then becomes a significant power source within the library. The problem really comes when the employee uses connections to intimidate you or to get in the way of the directions that you set. This is particularly difficult when you are the new kid on the block and don't have the credibility with these connections that the politically connected employee does. In short, the connections are going to believe your employee over you.

This is a challenge when you are engaging staff because the staff will know that there is a power struggle between you and the politically connected employee. They likely will side with you because people who use connections for ill are often problems in the workplace too. Siding with you is nice but regrettably does not solve the problem. A power struggle makes you look weak.

To be realistic, there isn't much you can do. Without kissing up, do have a good relationship with the employee while treading carefully, because everything you say will get back to his or her connections. Be watchful of what the employee is doing. Importantly don't give the employee any more power in the library than what he or she already has whether through positions or projects or important information or even more of your time than you would ordinarily spend with any other employee. Above all, don't think that you can turn around this employee by becoming a buddy and a friend. The objective of this employee is not friendship but power and the hope of having another director as a notch on the belt.

Remember that political connections don't last forever. Upper management moves on; elected officials term out. Importantly, begin to firmly establish your own network. Get yourself well connected so power can equal power. In the end, you still have to manage the library and there can only be one director. Do the job that you need to do and in the way that you need to do it. Staff need to see and to know that you are determined to build a positive environment regardless of the mischief caused by the politically connected.

Beware of the connections you do not know about. Universities and municipalities in particular can be inbred, and you might not know for a long time who is connected to whom and in what way. Therefore, be careful about what you say and to whom. As a director, your job depends upon your discretion. You are always on stage.

HELLO AND GOODBYE

The engagement of staff begins at the very beginning. The first interaction that a staff member has begins when the person applies for the position. A rapid response, polite letters or emails, courteous travel plans, a well-planned interview day, and cheerful welcomes all introduce the potential staff member to a library that is well run, purposeful, warm, and vibrant.

When the candidate is hired, be sure to be mindful of the new employee's introduction into the library. This begins the socialization process which introduces an employee to the values, behaviors, and expectations that you have of library employees. In addition to the orientation and training program that would be set up, don't forget the smaller things that send a message of welcome and respect. Can the employee select a new office chair, order supplies, or have a new computer? Was the office repainted or at least cleaned thoroughly? Does the new employee have a name plate on the office door or workstation before starting work? Is there a public welcome scheduled to which all personnel in the library are invited? Has a lunch been set up with you so you can get to know the person better? The transition to a new position is hard, but the new employee will greatly appreciate and long remember the warmth of welcome. Importantly, this employee likely will make an effort to be involved in a warm welcome to the next new person since these are the values of the library.

How we handle farewells also sends a message about our appreciation for the contribution that was made. Here is one thing to be mindful of. Employees vary greatly as to their expectations about how the library should celebrate their years at the library whether they have retired or resigned. Some want nothing; others want a public event. When we follow the individual's wishes, sometimes we get criticized for giving one person nothing while another gets a big event. Be clear with your staff that you always follow the person's wishes. In fact, this is best placed into the announcement about the person leaving. Use such phrases as "xx does not wish a retirement party, but your good wishes are very welcome" or "retirement party plans to follow." If aren't overt about this, the staff will come to think that you did have favorites after all—thinking that is not exactly conducive to the engaged environment that you are building.

Now, if you have an employee who has been fired or given the option to resign/retire or be fired, you likely will still want to announce that this employee has left the position—if there is no announcement, it creates an air of mystery as to why this employee has not shown up for the job. Remember that when there is a lack of information, people will create information, so you want to curtail too much gossip and speculation: there will be plenty of gossip anyway, since word about an employee in trouble always gets out.

Now, if you have terminated an employee who is hostile and combative or very disturbed, some staff may fear that the terminated employee will return to the library and retaliate with violence. Tragically, none of us anymore can ever rule this possibility out. Work closely with the police or security personnel so that they are aware of this situation. It helps also if a police representative comes to speak with the staff and talk about what police are doing and what the staff can do.

I think we have all seen announcements about an employee, whom we all knew to be a serious problem, which contained words of praise and thanks for his or her many contributions. We all wanted to ask: why did you fire the employee in the first place if he or she was that good? Staff are disheartened and puzzled if a problem employee is praised. Be consistent about your message—only engaged employees wanted here.

By the way, if you can't say anything in writing for legal reasons, you might still be able to do what is known as "strategic leaking." You tell a few people—I am presuming you already know who the best gossips in your library are—and let the news travel like wildfire. You might still be in for criticism by the staff that you did not formally announce that an employee is no longer at the library but this criticism passes quickly in the general relief of a problem being gone and the harmony of the workplace being restored.

CONCLUSION

This chapter covers a wide range of behaviors, actions, and attitudes. Just be mindful always of the impact that a director has on the workplace. You set the pace, you model the behavior, and you build the environment of engagement.

———

For more writings by me on this subject, see Managing the Interview, New York: Neal-Schuman, 1995.

Chapter Four

Dealing with a Board and the Faculty Senate

It is common for a library director to report not to one boss but instead to a board. This means there isn't one Customer Number One but five or even more. There are many, many variations of boards, such as elected or appointed boards of trustees, city councils, aldermen, town councils, councilors, selectmen, boards of supervisors, and so on. Even directors who do have only one boss can have advisory boards that are usually appointed by elected officials.

Some directors report to a mayor or a chief administrative officer but have to interact extensively with an elected board such as a city council. Directors in federal and state libraries may deal with committees on oversight and/or committees on appropriations.

In the case of universities, there is usually a faculty senate library committee elected by the faculty. This committee may also have student representation appointed by the student association. Universities also usually have boards of trustees and boards that govern fund-raising—the director may be called upon to make presentations to them about the library.

Likewise, directors of libraries that belong to museums or historical associations or other specialized libraries may also be called upon to make similar presentations to boards of trustees.

Given the presence and importance of boards in the life of a director, dealing effectively with boards of every type becomes an important skill for any library director.

Boards are along a spectrum of power. Some boards can hire, and fire, set policy, and determine budgets. Some boards are simply advisory to the director. However, no director should underestimate any board at any time. Any board can directly or indirectly affect budget and policies as well as public opinion about you and your library. Every board no matter how mild its role or demeanor must be taken very seriously.

No one chapter can detail how to interact with every type of board in every situation given the huge variations of types of boards and settings. Therefore, I am going to focus on best practices that will apply most of the time with most boards.

For brevity, I am going to use the term "board" to refer to the above bodies including the faculty senate library committee.

DEGREES OF CONTROL

Depending upon the nature of your board, you will have greater or lesser degrees of control over your board. Here is the basic rule: the more powerful they are, the less powerful you are. For example, if you have an advisory board, you will be the person who is setting the agenda. If you report to a city council, obviously you will not be the person who is setting the agenda but only submitting an agenda item. The point of this is for you to be aware of where your authority stops and the board's authority begins. If boards feel that you are intruding into their territory, they will have a range of reactions from feeling angry as in "who does that director think he/she is" to feeling disrespected to thinking that you are inexperienced for the job—none of these reactions make for a happy relationship with a board. Certainly some reactions may cause them to become more aggressive with you as they seek to put you in your place. Never overreach your authority where a board is concerned.

BASIC PRINCIPLES

Let's look at the basic principles of dealing with any board. I want to note at this point that all of the concepts about working with a boss apply here also. For example, if you directly report to a board, you would treat board members the same as you do a single boss. However, let's look at some differences, some points that are vital, that must be understood when working with a board.

Do your homework on board members. Understand their interests and their personal and career history. Be mindful of what businesses and properties they own. In the case of faculty, look at what research they are conducting, what classes they are teaching, and what consulting services they provide. Knowing at least these things will help you to understand their perspective on board agenda items and other library issues. This will also help you to keep your eye on any potential conflict of interest for board members.

For all types of boards, look for the connections between board members and other people, usually powerful, in the parent organization or community that surrounds the library. Pay careful attention to those connections. If your board is appointed, be aware of who supported each board member's appointment to the board. If your board is elected, pay attention to who came out in public support of whom. When you are working with board members, always remember that you are also "speaking" to the power or powers that are behind or with them.

Do treat all board members equally. While you will work closely with the chair of the board, you cannot afford to have favorites on the board even if inside you feel that way. Form no alliances with only one or two but instead alliances with all. Members on a board can detect easily if you are showing preferences. They will resent this behavior and consider that you are not supportive of them. If you are not supportive of them, they will not support you. Also, board members come and go. It may be that the person you favor the most will not be on the board again next term. Then you are left with the other members with whom you have a weaker relationship.

Inform all of them equally about any events or issues that concern the library. Never share information with one that you do not share with the others. Make sure they are all in the know. If the board is your boss, make sure you have weekly contact with each board member. Send them all weekly reports with updates about what happened in the library that week. It is also a good idea to send to board members reports, announcements, or issues about libraries in general. They will find it interesting and it will continue their education about the world of libraries. Of course, avoid the tendency of librarians to overwhelm people with information. Also, be careful how you transmit the information. Use layman's language and avoid the obscure jargon and acronyms of our profession.

Frequently new board members know very little about libraries. Consider how you might orient them to libraries. Some strategies, depending upon the type of board you have, include putting together a packet of information about the library, its history, and its governance; providing them with a job description that explains their duties and responsibilities; giving them a tour of the library in detail so they have a better understanding of its workings; or meeting with them one on one to go over some of the finer points of your library and libraries in general. Most board members will really appreciate an orientation because most board members are serious and professional and want to do a good job.

If you have new board members, consider if it is appropriate to have a welcome reception in the library. This is an opportunity for you to welcome them publicly, praise them for their coming service, and introduce them to the staff and to supporters such as major donors or members of the Friends of the Library. The board members will appreciate the public recognition and the chance to say a few words about their commitment to libraries, to students, to families, to children, to public service, to the community, and so on. Do ask the board members if they would like to have the press present or at least have a photo released to the newspaper of the board members at the reception.

If you have a board of trustees, one of the areas in which it is very important to educate new board members is related to confidentiality. Elected boards of trustees that have a lot of power also have a lot of access to confidential information particularly as it relates to personnel matters. Make sure that new board members know their responsibilities and the legal consequences if they violate confidentiality.

Do consider a strategic planning retreat again if appropriate to your type of board. Certainly at this point in your career, you can articulate a strong strategic plan for your library. Holding a retreat helps the board to come to their own understanding, to develop ownership over the plan, to deepen their knowledge of the issues of libraries, and to strengthen their commitment to the library's directions. You never want to spoon-feed a board with a plan—because then it is just your plan. A retreat helps board members to make the plan their own. Here is a heads up: watch where you have the retreat. Anything that smacks of luxury is a surefire way to get bad press.

In the same way that you will be loyal to any boss, be loyal to the board. Speak positively about them. Honor their dedication. Certainly, they have their own agendas for being there, but they are still being good citizens committing themselves to service.

When people are campaigning to be on a library board, do be careful not to get involved, however subtly you might think you are going about supporting certain candidates. If you take sides and you are on the losing side, you will be on the job market very quickly if you report directly to the board. Also be careful not to say anything privately about the elections either. Your opinion will likely be transmitted. Keep your thoughts to yourself. Now sometimes a candidate that you have known for a long time might ask you to come out publicly in support or to make donations. Usually and fortunately you are prevented from using your public role in any support of any campaign. As for private donations to a candidate, well, those often become public. Stay neutral; it won't earn you any friends but you won't get enemies either. One note, behind-the-scenes campaigning to be on the board can occur with advisory boards and faculty senators also. Again, stay silent; you don't want to have a rocky relationship with an advisory board or faculty senate committee either.

Margaret Donnellan Todd: "I think that public librarians need to understand two concepts: the quote attributed to Bismarck that it is best not to see how laws and sausages are made and the quote of Tip O'Neill that all politics is local. In other words, to succeed you need to understand politics and communities. Public librarians who do not master these two interrelated concepts will fail. Sometimes public librarians want to separate the 'pureness' of their service from the 'mess' of politics. That is not possible. Librarians must learn how politics works to ensure the support of elected officials. Since elected officials listen to communities, librarians also must understand the principles of community organizing. In my career, when an initiative was unsuccessful, 99 percent of the time it was because I failed to read the politics correctly or I failed to understand community dynamics."

If you are reporting to elected officials who have a larger portfolio than the library (such as a city council or board of supervisors might have), be realistic about where you are in their priorities. The library will never be as important in their minds as departments such as police and fire and will never carry that kind of weight and that kind of clout. Don't worry about your place in the hierarchy. Instead form alliances and friendships with these and other powerful department heads. In a later chapter, we will discuss the power of networks.

When you are new to the director's job, read and understand every law, regulation, rule, and charter related to your board. In particular in public libraries, boards are strictly governed and controlled by such documents. In academic libraries, the library committee is governed by the bylaws of the faculty senate. Those of you in overseas libraries may have to read up on the local laws of your host country too. If boards don't stay within the law, there can be many unpleasant results ranging from lawsuits to decisions invalidated, to bad press, to recalls, and so forth. While every board member has a responsibility to act within the law, you also are responsible as the chief officer of the library. And remember that whatever happens to your board happens to you. You won't get away unscathed. The board will look to you for your expertise and guidance in this area. So study well and become an expert. Of course, know your limits when giving an opinion—some matters are best left to attorneys.

Be aware that board members have their own agenda for being on a library board. For example, elected or appointed library board members often have political goals to higher elected office. Faculty senators may want to rise in the faculty senate, enjoy more power or prestige with fellow faculty, or come to the attention of administration in order to lay the groundwork for a management position. Your library board is not the end of any of their careers. Often a library board is the first stepping stone. This is also true of city council members with a large portfolio that includes the library. They often also want higher political office. Treat board members as the politicians that they are: their eyes are on votes, on future major donors to their campaign, on building powerful networks, and on winning issues that bring good publicity.

DEVELOPING THE AGENDA

As we discussed before, depending upon your board, you might be setting the agenda or you might be submitting agenda items. Regardless you are the one responsible for what items go to an agenda. Meet with your immediate staff and see what issues, projects, or concerns should come before the board over the next few months. While new things will always come up, you don't want to be scrambling month to month for agenda items. Regarding new things, do keep a list so that as issues emerge you have a constant reminder of items that may need to go to the board. It is surprising what we can forget in a busy week, and you don't want to be in a situation in which you have clearly forgotten to bring up an important issue.

One caution again: if you directly report to a board of trustees, remember your place. While you will greatly influence the agenda through items that you will recommend and behind-the-scenes conversations, be careful that you do not try to take control of the agenda. The board will eventually resent it. This is not a power struggle you want to be in.

Be completely knowledgeable about whatever subject is on the board's agenda. Sometimes with faculty senate committees or advisory boards, we can become very comfortable and even casual about the items on the agenda. This is when the mistakes occur. Take every agenda item very seriously because you never know what can be an explosive issue. Always do your homework and be ready for any discussion.

When presenting before any board, be objective in your presentation. Be positive and enthusiastic but without exaggeration. If you don't know the answer, say so, and then get back to them in a time frame agreed upon.

Always speak the truth even if the situation is very difficult or embarrassing or even exposes a flaw or weakness in your own management. Such situations only get worse. Every cover-up is eventually discovered and ends badly. Certainly, self-preservation kicks in and that is why human beings cover up things, but it is better to get it out in the open. Be honest and straightforward in all your dealings with the board. This is always a winning strategy.

Do your homework behind the scenes by communicating with each board member about issues before the public meeting. You should never come to an open meeting with new information. The board should know all already. This is not time for surprises. When they are surprised by information, it makes them look weak and it looks like you might be pulling a fast one or grandstanding. If you do this, know that you will hear about it not long after. Do this often enough to an elected board and you will be searching for a new position.

Do anticipate the position that the board members will take on the agenda items. Understanding their potential positions will help you to figure out what information is needed and how to lay the groundwork both in front of and behind the scenes for the public discussion.

Be comfortable with disagreements between board members and yourself. But don't become aggressive to prove your point. Be sensitive to all points of view. When a decision goes against you, remember you are there as a professional to advise. The decision finally belongs to the board if they have policy-making authority. If things often go against you, it is time to review what you are doing. It usually means that you are misreading the board members, their interests, and their agenda.

Also be comfortable with disagreements between board members. To live in a democracy means to be in endless conversations, disagreements, and controversies. If you anticipate a disagreement, be prepared to provide some alternatives or some compromises.

In particular in public libraries, there may be an audience attending a board meeting especially if there is a hot topic. When you are presenting to the board, pay little attention to the murmurings or comments from the audience. Some audiences can even become very hostile. Hopefully, the board chair will be controlling the audience, but don't let yourself get distracted and lose focus on your presentation and on the board's reactions.

When the time comes on the agenda for public comments, take note of any good points being made. Usually you won't respond to public comments unless specifically asked by the board either orally on the spot or later to them in writing. But if that doesn't happen, it is still likely that board members will follow up with you later casually on any good points so it will be useful to be prepared. Also take note of any well-connected person making comments. When you know the power and influence of opposing and supporting forces, it will help you to steer a controversial issue through the political minefields.

If you bring in an expert, make sure the expert is prepped and that you are fully familiar with what the expert is going to say. This expert could be a consultant, an architect, a person from another department working on a project with you, or one of your own staff. If the expert is inexperienced in speaking before a board, make sure that he or she knows the parameters of the presentation. Make sure the expert also knows the importance of deferring to you including never contradicting you in public and never trying to answer for you. Inexperienced people sometimes don't realize the political consequences of what they are saying. Sometimes also, being in front of a board goes to their heads and they start showing off or sharing information that is not appropriate. Be very careful about who goes before your board on behalf of the library. Choose people who are careful, mature, and steady and who will stay on the script.

Do keep your eye on subcommittees of the board. Some are doing important work, and you don't want to be taken by surprise by a subcommittee recommendation with which you do not agree. Fortunately if the work is vital enough, board members likely will invite you to join with them to provide expert knowledge.

You might also consider developing expertise on *Robert's Rules of Order*. This remains the foremost guide to parliamentary procedure. It is used by more boards than any other authority. Who can break a tie vote? What is a friendly amendment? Can proxy votes be accepted? How do items get on the agenda? What votes can be taken in executive session? These and many more procedural questions are answered in *Roberts's Rules of Order*. Debates about procedure can hold up agenda items. If you have a good working knowledge of this important book, you can solve a lot of debates about procedure among board members so that the agenda can keep moving along if appropriate for you to do so.

MAKING THE BOARD LOOK GOOD

You do want to think about how to make your board look good and how to give them opportunities to shine in public. Everyone on the board will appreciate that they have looked good in a public setting. There is an additional benefit to you and the library when board members look good publicly. They develop warmer feelings about the library. These feelings often carry over into all of their work on the board. Let's look at some ways to make the board look good.

One easy way is to make sure that board members have photo opportunities. Sometimes the student or local paper just wants a photo of something fun or interesting in the library. Let board members be in the photo instead of you.

Look for opportunities for board members to speak in public about the library. We all know what happens when we have to speak about a subject. We think about it, we learn about it, and we articulate it. In the process of developing a talk, we subconsciously make an internal commitment to the subject of our talk. Having board members speak in a positive manner about libraries means that they will bond more closely with the library.

For example, if the board is appointed by elected officials such as a city council, ask board members to speak to council about some issues. This doesn't mean that you disappear but give them a visible position from time to time. A politically connected board, which they usually are, can be a powerful voice for the library. Obviously, you will prep them so they don't get into deep water. And council will have already received a briefing package from you with the consent and knowledge of the board.

Now, if an agenda item relating to the library is coming up at an academic senate meeting, the chair of the library committee should speak to it with you there as an expert to respond to questions as needed. Not only will the library committee chair look good as the spokesperson but faculty speaking to faculty is more powerful than an administrator speaking to faculty. Of course, if you know that a controversial issue is coming up about the library, then it is a good idea for the chair of the library committee, with you in tow again as the expert, to meet in advance with the chair of the senate. The chair will appreciate having more background in order to manage the debate more effectively.

Some issues that will always be controversial for faculty include: a major reorganization that closes departmental libraries, the transfer of well-loved staff, reduction in funds for the collections, weeding the collection, inadequate journal collections, removal of parts of the collection to remote storage, slow document delivery, changes in the loan period for faculty, inadequate remote access to digital collections, and so on. Even though faculty are very preoccupied with their research, their teaching and the goings on of their departments, any controversial library issue can awaken these lions.

Again in a university setting, you likely will be giving the student senate an update on emerging issues, new projects, or programs a couple of times a year. In your remarks, be sure to recognize publicly the library committee student representatives and thank them for their contribution. Never forget the power of sincere and positive praise.

Here is another way to have board members look good: sometimes the library will be receiving important guests from another university, another city, or another country as examples. Or perhaps you are hosting a regional library workshop or seminar. Give the board members the chance to greet the guests and say a few words. Do give them some talking points. And again, invite the press.

If you have a professional conference coming up, do consider if any of your board members might be appropriate as a speaker and then work with them on crafting a speaker's proposal. Perhaps invite them to join with you as a speaker on a panel that you are developing.

If you are editing a book, consider if you want to invite faculty members on the board to write a chapter if the subject is relevant to their field. Faculty members often appreciate this since any scholarly work contributes to their CV for the tenure or posttenure process.

Naturally, if you have an important event such as a major program or a dedication, board members will be there visibly in the photos and on the platform. The board chair should always have a speaking role. If you report to an elected board, then the board chair may wish to take on the role of master of ceremonies. If your faculty senate library committee has student representatives, such events are a perfect occasion to give them an opportunity to speak on behalf of the library to fellow students.

Here is one tip: at ribbon-cutting ceremonies, make sure that your board members and you have your hands on the scissors. This is pretty much a guarantee that you will all be in the photo. While anyone can be cut out digitally, newspapers don't usually go to that bother when all the hands are on the scissors.

Finally, in helping your board to look good, there may be occasions when board members could be interviewed by the press about the library instead of you (or alongside of you). Of course, these will only be positive occasions: you want to make them look good after all. And, of course, you will meet with them beforehand and give them talking points that they can use. Also, give them some other information that they can just add in as appropriate such as the number of people who use the library in a single day, the most popular service, the impact that the library has on children or students or seniors, or perhaps a good story that illustrates the value of your library. Always provide them with something catchy about librarians or libraries nationwide. We will talk in another chapter about bad press.

BOARDS UNDER SIEGE

Sometimes boards are under siege because of decisions they made or are about to make. Decisions that will rile up the library customers include branch or departmental library closings, reduction in the budget for collections, journal cancellations, weeding the collection, Internet filtering, reduction in service or hours of service, reduction in children's services, and censorship. Anyone of these issues can become a hot button with emotions raging on both sides.

The best time to manage a controversial issue is before it happens. You already know what will trigger the customers, so if you are on the verge of proposing something that you know will be controversial, lay out a plan of action with the board behind the scenes. This plan should include the timing of when the issue goes public (if the timing is under your control), the rationale for the decision, the mode of presentation (reports, graphics etc.), and the opportunity for the customers to provide input through social media or other strategies. Never rush the process of input if you have a choice as people don't want to feel railroaded. If customers feel that they are not being heard, then it adds greatly to their emotions on an already problematic issue. Take the pulse of the people continually as their thinking will evolve on the issue. Read the comments on social media, in emails, and in letters. Understand their perspective. That knowledge will help you and board greatly as you steer through the issue. The bottom line is this: don't surprise your customers. Now, sometimes only the stark reality of a board's coming to a final decision wakes the people up, and then you have a small riot on your hands. Continue to provide the board, and the media, with the facts and with options. Only reason and time can overcome these challenges. However, don't be surprised if your board backtracks or delays a vote as a result of heavy public pressure.

Now in the case of budget reductions, which are so often the source of these unhappy discussions, you and your board might be tempted to propose draconian cuts in order to stir up the customers. This is usually preparatory to tax increases, a special tax for libraries, or to get the attention of a higher board that funds the library. Just remember that you are not the only ones playing that game—it is played at all levels. Everyone knows what you are doing. The danger is that there might be indifference to what you and your board perceive as unacceptable cuts. You could then be stuck with these cuts or have to backtrack in public. Naturally, credibility is lost, although, fortunately, people have short memories on these matters.

The irony with budget cuts is that everyone wants the library to continue providing everything even if statistics show clearly that the proposed cut is for a lesser used service. Libraries, even those not well used, seem to stir up emotions of what should be. The emotional attachment that people have to libraries is a good thing, but when it is aroused, community emotions can seriously affect sound management decisions about eliminating or reducing services that statistics show are not of interest to the community. Of course, if there are no emotions around the cuts being proposed, then there is a very serious problem in community interest and support of the library. It is time to relook at the library's relevance to the community.

It is a rare library that does not get involved in an issue involving the censorship of books and other resources. Censorship issues occur most in school and public libraries, but no libraries are exempt. Many excellent resources have been developed in the library literature regarding this topic, so I will not be covering that here. However, before a censorship issue is in front of your board, it is important for the board to know the current policies of the library regarding censorship and understand the reasoning and history behind the policy. Now a new board member upon seeing it for the first time might not agree with the policy and may wish to propose changes. This is just a risk you have to take because all board members have to know all policies.

Let's talk about your board and unions. If you report to a board that has the final say in contract negotiations, then it is likely that there will be union issues sooner or later.

If negotiations break down, the union may deploy a range of strategies to impact public opinion and library operations, including issuing press releases to the newspapers or television; utilizing social media; or devising work slowdowns, sick outs, strikes, and picketing. Your board might be completely under siege if negotiations go badly.

If appropriate, share with your board members the principles that we discussed in chapter 3. In particular, help your board to focus on these important points: remain centered and steady during these times, stay with the facts, explain the issues clearly and concisely in every setting, never criticize your employees, don't over-react to nasty comments in the press except to clarify misinformation, and never speak to anyone outside of the formal negotiating process in case key negotiating stances get leaked. Keep your board members focused on the fact that one day ugly negotiations will be over but all of you will still have a library to run. Now, some employees and unions won't make the high road easy for you, but you and your board members must be masters of your reactions to negative events.

Now sometimes unions will seek to divide you from the board. They might want to make you look like the bad guy in the hopes that you, one perceived roadblock, will be eliminated or neutralized. This may also give some scaredy-cat board members an idea so they can get the heat off of them and onto you. Just remember that you are part of a team with the board. You take actions with them and on behalf of them. Build that relationship from your first day with the board, and it is likely that they will stay strong with you.

Now for a different challenge: once in a while, a problem employee will lay siege to the board. He or she might request meetings with individual board members, write letters to the board, or speak during the public sessions. Usually this is the result of hostility toward you stemming from a personnel action which could range from not getting a promotion to disciplinary actions to being fired. And of course, there is just the unbalanced employee who wants to make trouble or sees him or herself as a crusader on behalf of the staff. Sometimes boards will accidentally encourage this by being sympathetic to start and then end up regretting that they ever indulged the employee.

Here are some strategies for curtailing this employee: keep your board (if you are a direct report) informed about personnel actions so there won't be any surprises; work with the board so that their response is neutral, which neither discourages a person from rights in approaching a public board nor encourages by asking questions or taking any action; and, if the board wishes to take an action, advise them to keep referring the employee back to you so the employee realizes eventually that there is no getting around you. Naturally you will be consulting with human resources so they can advise you as to the best course of action. If the employee is represented by a union, human resources can also speak with the union representative for a resolution. Be very careful throughout all of your actions that there is no hint of retaliation from you no matter how provoked you are, and it will be very provoking.

Worse, sometimes problem employees will partner together so you have not just one but two or more on your hand. If it gets to be more than one, the board is going to start being suspicious about your management style. So get on this problem fast before it gains a head of steam.

Sometimes in spite of everything that you are trying to do right, any discussion about any issue can take a deadly turn within the community of customers. If the issue gets too hot, the board might be looking for a fall guy. That would be you since you likely are the person who brought the issue forward or proposed the cuts or supported a policy. You can certainly end up pilloried by the board and the media. Additionally, some people, and the press, are always looking for issues on which to launch their own success. In spite of every reasoned proposal you might make, they see a hot button with which to stir up the community and earn them glory. Your best strategy here is to have the board deeply involved. Once again, make sure you are a part of their team and never a solo performer. Never take independent action or be too visible. If you do decide to champion a controversial cause for deeply held values, then at the same time, think about an exit strategy that protects you. We will talk more about exit strategies later.

BAD BOARDS

As the above example shows, there is a dark side to working with a board and things can go from being very challenging to getting very nasty. There are a wide range of scenarios regarding a board going bad. Let's look at the most common problems that will confront you.

Sometimes you just have bad luck and get board members with difficult personalities. These personality problems can have a wide range: the know-it-all who can't be told anything; the person, full of preconceived ideas, who has made up his or her mind before the information is in; or the big talker who is always pinning medals on his or her own shoulder.

The list does not stop there. What about the board member who won't let others get a word in; who has one axe to grind and does it continually in public; who is chronically unprepared for meetings; who doesn't seem to know or remember what is going on; who doesn't show up for meetings; who is scared of agenda items and keeps waffling for fear of offending anyone; or who brings up issues decided long ago.

And yet one more problem: the wild card board member. This is the person who is continually taking action separate from other board members. Perhaps the board has agreed on a direction but the wild card has just spoken to the press about a completely different direction. This wild card is usually in the business of self-aggrandizement or grandstanding for personal gain.

Frankly, these personality traits are so deep-seated that you have little choice except to live with it. Such unpleasant traits aren't going to be corrected by any action you take. Just tolerate it, don't let it get to you, be respectful in your behavior toward the offending board member, and keep on working in your usual fact-based, rational manner.

Do keep in mind that you aren't alone. The problem board member is also a problem to other members of the board. It is the responsibility of the board chair (who hopefully isn't the problem) to keep problem behavior in check at least in meetings. Other board members may also be supportive of the chair through their actions and responses. However, they often despair too when confronted with these difficult personalities.

Here is one strategy that might help a bit, but it assumes you have more authority over the agenda: consider increasing awareness of the right way to be a board member by encouraging your board to revise the rules and responsibilities of the board, update the board manual, and review the bylaws. Do provide training and development when the opportunity arises. For example, some of our professional conferences have workshops and meetings intended for library boards.

Now if you have an advisory board with a difficult problem member, you might want to work toward replacing him or her. Obviously the best time to do this is when the term of service is up. Watch out though—at the same time you are working to get a new person on the board, your problem member might be working to get reappointed. This isn't much of an issue unless the problem board member is powerfully connected. Just weigh the risks and decide if you want a better board or a powerful enemy. Also, when you are working behind the scenes to get a new member, don't kid yourself that you will be the hidden hand behind that action. These things are never confidential.

If you have a board that has been elected that is hostile to you or has been elected to get rid of you, it is already too late. Yes, it could occur that you could turn them around through serious conversations one on one, but by that time so much has happened and they probably have gone public on making management changes. From that position, they will have a hard time backing up as that will damage their own political career. As a director, you always have to have an exit strategy. If you see this coming, make your own exit gracefully. We will talk about this in a later chapter.

A board that is sharply divided is difficult to manage. This division could be caused by genuine philosophical differences about library service and library directions. It can also be caused by long-standing hostilities toward each other, which have nothing to do with the library. For example, faculty senators may have an issue with each other related to tenure or sabbaticals or research rivalry. Board divisions are often manifested by hostility in speech and behavior toward each other and continual bickering in public. Sometimes board members will deliberately take opposing votes because of personally disliking another.

In this situation, it is easy for the director to get buffeted from board member to board member. The best approach is to continue to treat each board member equally, to continue to stay rational in the midst of their emotions, and to continue to present facts about directions and problems that may appeal to their reason. Never expect to be the one who can reconcile a divided board. Do see if you can get the board chair to discuss with the board how the board wants to work together. Of course, some board members prefer to remain uncivil simply because of their personality or because it serves some agenda. If a divided or hostile board persists, do look for an exit strategy yourself because often as not they soon will begin to blame you for not solving the problem or for taking sides. Do look ahead and see when elections or new appointments will be made. If it is just a year, you can probably make it, but if you are looking at four years of this mess, it might not be worth it.

Camila A. Alire: "Leading libraries in a political context is an essential part of effective leadership. Every workday is political for library leaders no matter their library type. They need to be aware of the politics within their work environments—the library, the parent organization, and externally. By being politically astute, leaders learn how to handle themselves effectively when dealing with dynamic, challenging professional environments. Using power and influence effectively can determine their success as leaders."

Sometimes board members, and this is particularly true of faculty senators, can get bored with the agenda. A library is a very mature organization so there won't be major policy issues or new services to discuss on every agenda. Do engage them in issues such as strategic planning, significant shifts in collection development, or intellectual property—or some of the other great debates within libraries. Engage them in important decisions. Remember bored boards can turn destructive and angry at the most and just stop coming at the least.

Then there are board members that do not know the line between their role as a board and your role as the administrator. They are ignorant of sound management practices. As examples, they may continually butt into library business, try to manage the library, or try to give directions to your staff. If you report to the board, then this situation is tougher because they have more rights. If this is once in a while and minor, just shrug it off. However, if it is getting progressively more of a problem, you will have to talk with the board member who is crossing the line. Ask him or her to come to you directly if something is needed. Remind the staff that any interactions with the board over substantive matters must be brought to your attention. The more this goes on, the worse it gets. Some staff may begin to like working directly with a board member and the board member may begin to like directing the staff—getting gratification as a pseudo-director.

If the board chair is not the problem, you might want to discuss this issue with him or her. Possibly the issue could be addressed in general on the board agenda under the guise of board roles. No matter how it is handled, it will be an awkward situation. The problem board member, who clearly doesn't know boundaries in the first place, won't be pleased at having his or her behavior criticized, curtailed, or thwarted however subtly this is handled. I know you won't be surprised if the behavior continues.

Now, if you have micromanagement by several or all board members, you might want to look at your own management. Why do board members want to do an end run around you? Are you contributing in any way to this problem? Has the board lost confidence in you?

One of the worst situations is the board member who is not truthful with you, with the public, or with other board members. If you suspect that you have such a person and it can take a while to detect, just keep a close eye on them especially around any personnel, legal, or fiscal matters. When board members lack a commitment to truth, they can cause damage in many areas.

Sometimes an elected board member is abusing or is attempting to abuse fiscal responsibilities. It is surprising what can occur when it comes to money. This is another problem that is better solved before it occurs by constantly watching the dollars, making sure that all of the controls are in place, reporting accurately, and being frank about any problems. If problems do occur, then you do have to report this clearly.

Most boards know that they have to work closely with and in support of more powerful boards. For example, a board of public library trustees should be mindful of the greater power of a city council. However, sometimes a board can get the bit between their teeth and create a conflict with a more powerful board. Often this occurs regarding funding. Your board might be upset or angry about the level of funding for the library. It is one thing for a board to deploy a strategy that appears oppositional to a more powerful board in order to garner support for the library. It is quite another for one board to make hostile, critical, or offensive comments about another. Slinging mud in public helps no one and especially not the library. If this occurs, express your concern privately to your board members and help them to understand that such hostility will hinder the library's mission. Make every effort, in public and in private, to speak positively and respectfully about both boards. Be the voice of reason.

Sometimes, board members begin to see you and the staff as servants. They ask for personal favors, space, use of library vehicles, inappropriate use of meeting rooms, or other favors that you would not do for customers. Of course, while you do go the extra mile for board members, there is still a line that cannot be crossed. Some of these requests may violate regulations, as public goods may not be used for private gain. Unfortunately, you will have to discuss this directly with them—explaining the issue and the consequences of using public goods.

CONCLUSION

No matter what type of board you work with, always be prepared, be aware, and never underestimate the power of individuals or the group on a board. Do be mindful that in any of these scenarios, if they get out of control, you can be sacrificed. This doesn't mean you should act with fear but always be mindful to be on top of your work with any board.

Chapter Five

Dollar Sense

This chapter addresses what every library director should know about managing the library's financial resources. Any mismanagement of money, no matter how innocent, can get a director into deep trouble very quickly. So let's spend some time with the key points that will enable you to manage the library's budget effectively.

THE BREADWINNER

It is important for directors to be clear about their role regarding money. The simplest way to describe it is that you are the breadwinner. It is your responsibility to make sure that the library has adequate resources to do its job. Now this is easier said than done, since an economic downturn will greatly impact the library's budget. Over this type of situation the director has little control. Regardless, the staff will look to you to make sure that the library has resources. Bring in money, and you are deemed successful. Have huge budget cuts, especially if they are disproportionate to the other parts of the parent organization, and you are deemed weak and without power.

Now, here is the point where you need to be careful. When you have one good year of a strong budget, don't crow about it to your staff. That one good year is often followed by a not so good year. What you claim as a success you must also claim as a failure too. Budgets are cyclical, but you don't want your reputation as a leader to be cyclical too.

A successful breadwinner has these characteristics: a good relationship with the boss, effective customer service leading to satisfied customers, a well-developed network of supporters, an effective fund-raising program, supportive elected officials, excellent marketing that always tells the library's story, an engaged staff, a strong personal image born of professional success and the regard of peers, and a forward-looking library that delivers regularly on its goals. Hit as many of these points as possible and you will have done as much as can be done to be a successful breadwinner.

KNOW THE DOLLARS

It is vitally important that a director really know the dollars. Most of our graduate programs will give us only rudimentary information about managing a budget. You must be engaged in your personal on-the-job training and learn as much about budgeting as you can.

Certainly, directors of all but the smallest of libraries have staff who manage the budget. A good budget manager will handle the accounting, provide budget projections and sound advice, and partner with you in developing financial strategies. However, no matter how good a budget manager you have, the final management of the budget is the responsibility of the director. You are the one who decides how the money is allocated.

Think about the budget this way: You are responsible for the library's plans, directions, services, goals, projects, and so on. You are the one who is responsible for the priorities of the library. A budget provides financial support for all of these efforts. How can you achieve what you want to achieve unless you are the person who is directing where the money will go? Given this, it is therefore very important that you know the dollars. If you don't know enough about what is going on with the budget, how can you make critical decisions about where the money goes?

Be careful in particular when you are a new director. Three things can happen. First of all, when you start, you don't know where all the funds are or what their history is. Government budgeting in particular can be very convoluted. Spend time with your budget manager, look at the past history of the budget, make sure that you understand what every pot of money is—especially the "soft" funds that might be the result of fund-raising. Don't delay on learning the budget.

Second, when you first start, you might face resistance as to your "intrusion" into the budget. People can get very territorial, and there is no better opportunity for mischievous persons to establish power than when a new director comes on board. One way that this manifests itself is when you get inadequate information about the budget. You might ask for a full report and get a few lines. You might ask for a monthly report and only get part of the budget. Don't accept less than comprehensive information. Month in and month out, you should have a full and detailed budget report. How can you manage the money unless you know what is happening?

Finally, as a new director, you might be walking into a fiscal mess. If that is so, dig into the budget and clean it up right now. If you wait, then you will be blamed for the budget mess. You have one year at the most to clean up budget problems, so get on it. Of course, let your boss know the situation.

Now, sometimes, you will have managers who, under the pretense of being concerned about your busy schedule, will offer to take the responsibility of the budget from your shoulders. Don't fall for that. Control of fiscal resources is power. People will go to the person who knows and controls the dollars. Never give control of the budget to others. Never abdicate your role in fiscal management if you want to stay in a leadership position.

Make sure that your managers also become knowledgeable about the library's budget. Do involve them in high-level budget planning and management. When your managers become knowledgeable about the needs of the other units of the library, they make more of an effort to work together and to support each other. Your goal for your managers is for them to think about the library and its needs overall and to provide you with budget recommendations that are not rooted completely in territoriality. They can't do that unless they have full budget information. While managers will still fight for their units, the infighting will be reduced as understanding of other needs is increased. This means you will spend more of your time having a rational budget discussion as opposed to contending with the gamesmanship and maneuvering, which, however subtle, is a hallmark of many budget discussions.

> *Rod Hersberger*: "No matter the kind of library, the director better know a good deal about budgeting, finance, and accounting. Formal courses are always useful in gaining this knowledge. It is also very important to be able to relate to higher management how adequate funding supports the library's programs, services, and collections (knowledge resources). Just saying we need more money is not effective. Don't whine about what you don't have, but demonstrate how effectively you are employing all resources at your disposal."

As a director, you have to make sure that your staff has confidence in you regarding fiscal matters. Do speak about the budget, release information about it, and let people know what is going on. This puts you at the center as a source of information regarding fiscal matters and shows your knowledge and control. Staff drop clues when they don't have confidence in you regarding the budget. If your staff are endlessly fussing about the budget, endlessly asking questions, endlessly challenging decisions, then you probably have a credibility issue. It is true that you might have an agitator on your staff, but you should be able to detect if that is the source.

On the other hand, don't be endlessly talking about the budget and the lack of it. This only depresses people and makes them disengage from the library. You might find that good staff start to look at their options elsewhere. You may find that staff begin to reduce their expectations of the library. Their commitment to excellence begins to wither. After all, what is the point of going on? While you want your staff to be informed, the burden of cutbacks must fall onto you. You are the one who has to shoulder the challenges.

Just remember this: the budget is your responsibility. Establish yourself as a director who is very knowledgeable about the budget.

MANAGE THE DOLLARS EFFECTIVELY

The word, "effectively" implies success. In order to be a successful director, you have to manage the budget successfully. Let's look at some of the components of success.

Laurel Patric: "Every library director should know that flexibility is a virtue. With libraries changing daily, the path from idea to implementation is never a straight one. Flexibility is not thoughtless mind changing or the inability to reach a decision, but it is being ready to rethink priorities, change direction, and move the end point as necessary. This goes for building projects, budgeting, personnel, programming, collection development, and whatever else crosses your desk. Knowing that flexibility is a daily part of the job makes being a library director easier and so much more fun."

Make sure that you have a three-year budget projection. Of course, many things happen to a budget, which means that there is never any certainty, but a three-year projection helps us to make long-range decisions. For example, if you know you need a major technology purchase or a facility upgrade, then planning to store money, if you can, toward that purchase over three years is a sound approach.

Be wary of the mid-year point in the budget. This is a time when a possible surplus, a possible shortfall, a mid-year cut, or a mid-year increase can occur. Never be caught without a plan for these fiscal upturns and downturns. Always have a plan that is vetted by your team. If we are cut, we do this. If we have a surplus, we do that. Being caught without a plan is a surefire way to either spend the money less wisely or make cuts less wisely.

Really understand what people need. This seems obvious, but it is surprising how sometimes a director can learn much later, after the budget is allocated, that one unit really needed some major equipment. Sometimes staff just don't think about their needs in time. This is why it is a good idea to give people plenty of warning when they can submit their requests. This is why it also makes sense for you to walk around and talk to all of the staff and supervisors throughout the year and make note of any particular needs. You also will spot things yourself that they might not have thought of.

After allocation, make sure it is spent. Procrastination and human nature go together, so you do need firm cut-off dates for when certain funds must be expended. Usually your parent organization will have those due dates anyway, but you don't want your budget to have year-end surprises by people not ordering what has been approved. This is another reason to review a monthly budget, which will show outstanding expenses.

Do consider centralizing more of the budget. This will eliminate territoriality ("that budget belongs to my unit only") but of course competition, which always exists with resources, will remain. Centralizing is more effective in a bad budget year, since you can move resources more easily to those that need it without the supervisors and managers tussling with you over "taking" their budget to use for another area. Centralizing can also save money because in a decentralized budget people will always spend up to whatever they have for fear of "using it or losing it."

Let's talk about the political dimension of managing effectively. First, be fully aware that resentment and anger can build in any library over who gets what and how much of the library budget. For example, normally you would think that a new position would be celebrated in the library. It will be, but only by those who got the position. Every other unit will be wondering why it isn't theirs. After all, don't you have the same emotions about another department or college or unit who got more positions than the library?

This is one reason to make sure that the budget is transparent. Your budget decisions might be fair, but if no one knows about them, there will be the impression of money being hidden or favorites being played. Have a budget review once a year for the staff. This will help them to get rid of the emotions around a budget and instead look at the facts. People can have a lot of mischievous opinions about the budget so getting the facts in front of everyone helps to counter that. In particular, it might help to get rid of that common assumption that administration has a golden pot of dollars stashed somewhere.

Do be very careful about your personal expenditures. Don't go to every conference. Don't have your office redone when other library units are desperate for equipment and furniture. Don't be the first one to get a computer upgrade. Always put the needs of the whole library first. People will be too ready to assume that you are putting yourself first anyway. Be especially careful when you are a new library director. Getting first dibs on the budget toward your personal needs will send a clear message that you are selfish.

Do watch very carefully that vendors deliver on contracts. The newspapers are full everyday of some organization that has a significant cost overrun on a contract which, by the way, is always accompanied by a failure to complete the job. Yes, it might cost the vendor, but it will cost you far more. It makes you look completely ineffective, and in fact, it would be true. Be particularly wary of any contract involving technology and facilities. They have very high costs and very uncertain delivery dates.

If a serious mistake has occurred in the budget, such as much less than was anticipated or a discovery of new monies when you have been complaining about shortages, correct the problem as soon as possible. If the mistake is large, let your boss know what happened, how it was corrected, and what controls you have in place for the future. Your staff may have goofed, but the problem is yours. Of course, you will be keeping a much closer eye on your budget manager for the time being until you are comfortable that the problem will not reoccur.

If the budget process allows, do retain contingency funds. Major facility needs such as a leaking roof or expensive technology failures and so forth can happen at any time. Some of these might be covered by the parent organization, but even then it often is charged back to the library's budget. Have some funds on hand to cover these sudden unplanned expenses.

While you must be conservative about the budget, don't be afraid to take risks either, for example, with some new revolutionary technology or a brand new service. Just calculate the risk. What is your chance of success? If you fail, what will you lose? Here, keep in mind our discussion on downstream thinking.

WALKING THE STRAIGHT AND NARROW

At the outset of your administration, be clear with everyone that you walk the straight and narrow where the budget is concerned.

Never waver and never compromise. We already talked about the importance of being values driven. If you are values driven, you won't compromise your values, and honesty in fiscal matters is an important value. If you start compromising, then your staff may also—after all you have already established that you have a lower bar for honesty. This will corrode the culture of the library in time. Also, need I say that any suspicion regarding honesty in fiscal matters is the beginning of the end for any library director?

Being honest in fiscal matters can take many shapes. As you steer the library on the straight and narrow path, keep your eye out for some of these problems: diverting donated funds into purposes other than the donor's wishes, diverting grant monies into purposes other than requested, sweeping a fiscal problem under the rug, padding travel expense accounts, fudging mileage reimbursement requests, purchasing collections more related to personal interests than community need, utilizing the photocopier extensively for personal use, receiving funds to attend a conference but not attending the meetings, making personal international calls on the company phone, working a business on the side on company time, or using the library's vehicles or equipment for personal use. It is surprising what people can get up to in an organization. Correct these problems immediately.

Don't use the budget as a tool for dark power. Allocate money fairly and transparently without regard for personal favorites. Don't reward and punish through the budget. We already talked about being a mafia boss. If the unit needs the money, it needs it regardless of how you might feel about the unit's supervisor. And never use the budget as a reason to prevent change. A budget should facilitate, not obstruct. Certainly, there are things that you cannot and never will be able to afford. That is different from deliberately using the budget as an excuse because you don't want to make that change.

Watch what you sign. Particularly when you are new, forms will come at you fast and furious. Make sure you know what those forms are and what they do. Particularly be careful around contracts. When a 200-page contract hits your desk, it is tempting just to rely on the experts. Make sure that you are clear on what the contract says and what you are committing to. Don't just pass that contract off to someone else because it is too long or too technical to read.

Do provide budget training to anyone who also manages their local budget. No matter what the staff does with money, you are the one who is responsible. Stress the ethics as well as the procedures. Make sure they understand what they are signing. Also make sure that they know their limits in terms of what they can approve and what they can commit to fiscally. Having to reverse a financial commitment or disapproving what has been approved by a supervisor who went beyond his or her limits of authority and agreed to what should have not been agreed to is always difficult. It results in upset employees and possible grievances.

Keep an eye on volunteers. Cash can go through the Friends of the Library through various book sales and programs. The Friends have to have the same fiscal controls as the library. This is harder when they are set up as a separate entity, which usually happens with public libraries. Make sure you are on the board, reviewing the money carefully, and raising issues and concerns publicly. You are the one who is going to get the black eye if anything goes wrong.

Do study any rules, regulations, or laws concerning conflict of interest. Getting into a conflict of interest can have legal implications from bad press to a fine to jail time. This will also mean that you will lose your job, your good name, and possibly your career. Nothing is worth that. Particularly be careful when you are a new director as it is easy to walk into a conflict of interest without realizing it. Watch out for meals from vendors, gifts, honorariums, supported travel, or personal discounted deals. Be very mindful of your relationship with all vendors—current and potential. Vendors do want to get cozy with you because that is a way of doing business, but it is your responsibility as to where you draw the line. Of course, make sure that all staff who have fiscal responsibility or who sign contracts have conflict of interest training. Whenever you have doubts about anything being a conflict of interest, you had best err on the side of caution. Here is one gauge: if you don't want to read about it in the newspapers the next morning, then don't do it.

Now, be very straightforward to your boss about money. Money brings out the gamesmanship in us all. Frankly, there isn't any game with money that you can play that your boss doesn't know about. Keep in mind how much experience in organizational life your boss has. If you are caught out in any game related to money, and you will be, it will cause your boss to lose trust in you. This is not a position that you want to be in.

Need I say that your own staff might be thinking about playing games with you too? Just let them know that there isn't any game that you don't know. Make sure that everyone walks the straight and narrow.

THE BOSS AND MONEY

It is inevitable in any career that the boss comes to the library looking for money. Perhaps the boss is cutting the budgets of every unit. Perhaps the boss is just targeting the library because other units are politically too difficult to cut, such as police and fire, or too powerful, such as revenue and enrollment generating at a college. Perhaps the boss has seen that you have soft monies that are as yet unallocated.

In reality when a boss explicitly requires funds from your library, there is little you can do at that moment. The secret to success lies in preparation before any directive is given. Make sure that your boss always knows the needs of the library; make sure that your boss is aware of the impact if the library's budget is reduced. Importantly, make sure that any large amounts of soft money are always allocated and that the boss knows about it. For example, you might be saving for a new OPAC or for some high-end equipment or to make some facility changes. Obviously, these items should also be a priority of the boss and of clear benefit to your customers, otherwise those soft funds will disappear in a wink into the boss's coffers.

Often the boss will not be explicit with you about seeking to remove funds but instead the boss's budget people will carry out the boss's orders. You always will have a heads-up when questions out of the ordinary come from the boss's budget people to your budget people. This means clearly that they are sniffing around your budget. This is a good reminder that the boss's budget people should also know the library's priorities and intents. Their knowledge might not save your budget, but sometimes the impact can be reduced.

It is very hard when money is taken from the library. You and your staff had your heart set on using it for specific purposes and you were diligent in husbanding your resources. Losing money to your boss is no reward for sound fiscal management. Moreover, it is also hard not to take it personally and hard not to be angry. There is always a feeling of failure when funds are taken away even if the economic situation clearly warrants it. Worse, sometimes you find out that the funds were not spent wisely or that the boss had a financial surplus at the end of the year. Here is one tip to ease your natural upset: just remember that you are the steward of the library funds, not the owner.

GETTING AUDITED

Auditing is a routine process as it ensures that the library is in fiscal and legal compliance. But while it is routine, it can never be taken casually because any problems with the audit can create serious legal, public relations, and financial situations for you and the library. Here are some tips to remember when the auditors come.

First, auditors are not on your side. They work for the parent organization.

Second, provide auditors only with the information that they request. This does not mean that you are covering anything up, but there is no reason for them to be free-ranging through the library.

Third, answer only the questions that they put to you. This is not a time to be chatting on about every issue and problem that you have. If you do, the auditors will follow every possible trail and you may have them with you for months.

Fourth, if the staff is talking to the auditors, make sure that they have the same political savvy that you have.

Fifth, be scrupulously honest. Auditors have built-in radars for problems.

Sixth, watch out for big game hunters. Not all auditors are nice guys, and some want to make their reputation on any problems that they might find.

Seventh, remember that auditors don't know libraries. Take time to explain your practices and make sure they understand why you do what you do. Otherwise, they will come to faulty conclusions.

Eighth, when you get their recommendations for changes, don't hit the ceiling but instead look at their concerns and make thoughtful responses.

Ninth, make the changes that are required. If the same problem shows up in next year's audit, your boss will call you to account.

Tenth, when a negative report goes public, let a representative from the parent organization speak to the press—most organizations have public relations people who are far more skilled in managing negative press. If you have to speak to the media, speak in the most positive fashion. Express appreciation that these issues were brought forward so you can continue to safeguard public funds. Explain how the library is moving forward to address the problems.

Eleventh, keep your boss in the loop if there are any problems surfacing.

Now, if you are running a library that has an independent budget, likely you and your board will have more control over the auditors because you are the client. You still want to run a clean house but you will have more control over the recommendations and when and where the recommendations are available.

A library can also have a nonroutine audit because of suspected embezzlement, theft of library goods, or theft of cash at the services desks as examples. Sometimes these crimes are detected by someone in the parent organization, discovered in a routine audit, or spotted by your alert staff. Theft must be reported both to the auditors, to the police, and to your boss. It is a big headache coming, and your management practices will be called into question (by yourself as well), but just go forward. Get it cleaned up. Put the controls in place for the future. Get better training for the staff. Resist all temptation from your inner voice and your staff to just sweep these problems under the rug. Again, this goes back to walking the straight and narrow.

MANAGING TIME

It is an old saying that time is money but it is so true. Therefore, to be fiscally responsible we do have to be very aware of how time is spent in the library.

Now, one of the biggest of time wasters is meetings. Do use best practices when it comes to meetings and encourage other managers and supervisors to do the same. Best practices include meetings that have a clear purpose, an agenda sent out ahead to attendees, an on-time start and finish, and minutes that expressly note follow-up actions. It is worthwhile spending some of your time learning the best way to manage effective meetings.

Watch out for a culture of lateness in the library. If you add up the lost time, it can have a significant impact on the productivity of the library. It may have become acceptable for staff to be chronically late for work, take longer breaks, and drift back from lunch. You don't have to become a martinet but make sure your managers are on top of this issue. It is a hard problem to correct, so you do have to keep up the needed pressure. You can't just address this issue once and then forget about it. When you are a new director, you can lay it out that one of your expectations is that people get to work and return on time. Of course, you and your fellow managers must set the pace and always be on time yourselves.

Usually, there will be some employees who will routinely waste your time by talking too much in any meeting with you. Sometimes employees with this problem are naturally talkative, unable to pick up well enough on body language to know when a conversation is over, always overriding the needs of others, or letting access to power go to their heads. Once in a while is okay, but if it happens routinely you do have to keep them from settling down and getting comfortable in your office. Now, if you don't have a secretary who can discretely interrupt a meeting that has gone on too long, then use these strategies when they come to your office: stand up and keep on standing, or take them out of your office for a walk to discuss the issue. You will still be able to accomplish what you need to accomplish with the meeting but it will be easier to conclude the meeting when you are not sitting down comfortably in your office. It is also a good idea to have a clock in your office which faces your guests so that they can also monitor their own time. It won't work with the ones who don't respond to subtle cues but it will help generally.

Watch your own time. So many little things can crowd the day and at the end of the week, we realize that we have not accomplished one thing on our list. Become a student of time management and use such best practices as making a to-do list the night before and tackling major goals first thing in the morning.

EMPLOYEE TURNOVER

Sometimes we worry more than we need to about employee turnover. There is an assumption that employee turnover means that we are not running a good library because people are leaving. That concern is only legitimate if you have high and consistent turnover or if you hear the same reason for leaving over and over again in the exit interviews. Ordinarily, turnover isn't a bad thing because it brings in new people with new ideas, creates opportunities for change, and frees up money.

Now, certainly there are people whom we want to retain. Their contribution and skills are exceptionally valuable. But at the other end of the spectrum, there are a few people whom we are downright glad to see go.

Regardless, a vacancy is always an opportunity. You can change the position substantially, reallocate it, upgrade it, and so forth. Also, you can usually retain the salary dollars that can be used for other things until the position is filled. For example, salary savings can be used for one-time large purchases such as computers, furniture, equipment, and so on. Make sure though that you don't start funding operations on salary savings because when you fill that vacancy you will have to cut operations. Do consider that if you keep the position vacant too long, you might signal to your boss that you do not need the position. In fact, if the position can be vacant for a long time, you have to ask yourself if the position is needed. Now, your boss might seize monies derived from vacant positions, so there is no advantage to you to not move forward and fill the position.

Now what about an employee who interviews for a job in another library and gets a higher salary offer? There are two responses that you can make—one, if you wish to retain the employee, then counter with an attractive offer. The employee might still accept the other position for a variety of reasons, but still you did your best to retain a good employee.

Two, if you don't wish to retain the employee, then remain silent. There is no need to take any action. Of course if the employee was engaged in the game of securing a job offer in order to get a pay raise from you, you will have an angry employee on your hands. After all, could there be any clearer signal about an employee's status when you make no effort to retain him or her?

CONCLUSION

The message of this chapter is to be very attentive to the money. Not only will allocating the money appropriately get you where you want your library to go, but it will also keep you out of serious trouble.

———————

For more writings by me on this subject, see "Survivor: The Library Edition," *Library Journal*, Vol. 134, No. 6, April 1, 2009; http://www.libraryjournal.com/article/CA6645870.html?nid= 2671&rid=##reg_visitor_id##&source=title (accessed April, 13, 2009); "Fund-Raising: The True Story," *LJXpress*, May 13, 2008. http://www.libraryjournal.com/article/CA6560383.html (accessed May 13, 2008); "Budget Shortfalls: A Survival Guide," *Library Journal*, May 15, 2003; "Scope, Timeline and Budget" in a book entitled *Developing Web-Based Instruction: Planning, Designing,*

Managing and Evaluating for Results. Edited by Elizabeth Dupuis and Cheryl Laguardia, New York: Neal-Schuman, 2003. Also published by Facet in London under the title *Planning, Designing and Assessing Online Learning*.

Chapter Six

The Borders of the Realm

Let's just start with a basic principle that every library director should know: you can never have too many friends. A director needs many friends in places high and low and far and wide.

A library, and therefore a library director, while valued and important, is rarely innately powerful. Your job is to increase your power, because the more powerful you are, the more likely you are to achieve your goals for the library. A strong network of friends increases your personal power—the power of the well connected.

In addition to power, how else will a strong network benefit you? Here are a few benefits: new information, good advice, revitalizing ideas, project opportunities, a sounding board, camaraderie, favors, future jobs, suggestions for talented employees, and the good public relations resulting from people who know and like you.

Certainly the main focus of a director is managing the library, but we ignore at our peril the important domain of building a network. Every director should be a member of or actively outreach to a larger community of organizational and professional peers, clubs and associations, and library supporters. In order to be a successful director, you continually have to work beyond the borders of the realm of the library, that is, beyond your four walls. You have to manage your relationship with this larger community in order to build and sustain your network.

The alternative to networking, and building your power base, is to be in a bubble—isolated. No director can afford to be cut off from others. This is the way to be forgotten, irrelevant.

Now, this means that you will spend a lot of time on your job facing outward and incorporating yourself into the life of many communities of interest. As with everything in management, this is not without its challenges. Now, let's look at the things every library director needs to know about networking.

> ***Elizabeth Martinez:*** When I started out, I wish I had known . . . "the difficulty for librarians to step out of a box and into community-based work with people outside the library, the sense that librarians must be infallible, therefore so much attention to 'what if' concerns, the expectation that the public would conform to the profession not the other way around."

A FRIEND INDEED

In this section, I want to focus on our relationship with our organizational peers—by which I mean those who hold equivalent positions in the parent organization. For example, if you are a public library director, it means other agency heads. If you are a university librarian, it means the deans of the colleges. If you are a special or corporate librarian, it often is other unit/department heads.

There are three things that are particularly challenging when trying to build a network and be a friend in organizational life. First, we have to continually have a generous viewpoint. It isn't easy when peers are getting facility upgrades, new technologies, additional staff, awards, and so forth. Jealousy often raises its head, and jealousy is a powerful emotion. You see this and you want it for your library too. Look at this instead as an opportunity to cement your friendship. This is a time to praise the successes of your peers. Congratulate them and celebrate their achievements. You know how you would feel if the roles were reversed, so be an unjealous friend.

Second, help your peers out. Maybe there is a project that requires some assistance. Maybe there is a grant that needs some research. Maybe there has been a tragedy that has impacted their unit. Be there for people. Offer your help. They will appreciate your support. To have friends means that we have to be a friend.

Lastly, do be kind to people in their troubles. A lot of bad things can happen to us in organizational life and not all of it is within our control. When peers are in trouble, this is not a time to sit back and enjoy the process. You don't have to come to their defense if they got themselves into hot water, but a kind word, a smile, or understanding is vital. They won't forget it. Remember too that you could be there yourself one day.

One footnote: when relating to peers, do keep in mind that one of them might one day be your boss. A dean of a college could rise to a provost, a department head to a city manager or a chief executive officer, and so on. Now is a good time to build a positive and productive relationship. Not only will this bring immediate pleasure in having a great relationship with a peer but it will yield benefits in the future too if the peer becomes your boss.

NETWORK VERSUS CLIQUE

While a successful director needs to build a strong network, it is important not to become a diehard member of a clique. A clique sends a message of exclusion—there is an in crowd and everyone else. Yes, it is emotionally rewarding to be part of an in crowd in the same way it was in high school. The popularity, the closeness, and the power of a group can be very enjoyable, but no director can afford to send any message of exclusion to others.

Sometimes we just land in a clique regardless because of chemistry between people. You are just part of a group that gets along well. You all connect with each other. You have similar values and attitudes. However, never rely on just one group for your power. Cliques are not forever. For example, members of your clique will leave for other jobs. If you haven't built up your network outside of the clique, you could find yourself isolated. Or perhaps your clique was well connected to your boss, but now you have a new boss and power has shifted to another clique. If you have been relying exclusively on your clique for power, you might find yourself on the outside looking in. Also pay attention to the resentment of people who are not in the clique—especially if your clique is a powerful one. Sometimes, outsiders are upset about being out in the cold and strive to damage the credibility of people in the clique.

Regardless of whether you are in a network or a clique, don't kid yourself about how strong your network or your clique really is when you are in trouble. It is important to remember that most friendships related to work are economic affiliations and should not be confused with deep personal friendships. If you are in trouble and it looks like you are going down for the count, never be surprised that your now former friends will keep their distance. They are engaged in their own organizational survival and will not want to be tainted by you. In short, never think that you are completely protected by any network or clique.

THE DANGER ZONE

Everyone knows that working with people can be hard. Day in and day out, we have to work with people whom only the organization has put together. We might be very dissimilar in our behavior, characteristics, and values. Networking with people can try our patience daily.

How will you handle a peer who is critical of the budget allocated to your library? Your peer might comment casually by saying, "Why do we need libraries anymore? Isn't everything on the Internet?" A peer who says this once provides us with an opportunity to educate about the true role of libraries. But if this peer makes this or similar comments about the library's budget, future, and role more than once, you likely do have someone who is interested in a reallocation of some of the library's budget. This means that in spite of all of your networking, you have a fight on your hands. However, don't have a hair trigger when someone attacks the library. Instead, analyze your opponent. Why is your peer doing this? Why now? What is the true agenda? Is it really just about the budget? What does your peer have to gain? Actions flow from desires, so you must figure out what it is that your peer desires. Once you know the person's motivation, you can begin to develop a strategy to respond. And respond you must before this peer begins to create a groundswell.

Be wary of the person who is the attack dog for the boss. Perhaps he or she has "read" that the boss actually wants to do such and such with the library but the boss doesn't want to do the dirty work because it is something that you might oppose. Before you react to any situation, think about it and look to see if there is the unseen hand of the boss behind the attack dog's comments. How can you detect the unseen hand? Think back about past conversations with your boss. Often, there are clues there. Were there casual questions about the directions of the library, suggestions for new goals or references to something another library is doing? These conversations might have occurred so casually that you never understood them as directives and therefore never acted on them.

Do ask the boss directly what he or she thought about the comment or comments by the person who was carrying on the attack. Ask this casually. A boss usually will be quite relieved to have the issue in the open. In the future, remind yourself to pay more attention to what the boss is saying.

Remember too that attack dogs really want to ally themselves with power so they also can misread the situation in their eagerness to please. Don't read too much into it yourself, but, again, never let negative comments about the library stand.

Be wary of the peer who works behind the scenes, who is charming to your face but stabbing you in the back. It can take a long time to figure these people out, but they will be detected by you eventually. The existence of such people is one reason why you must always be careful about what information you share.

Don't avoid those who intend mischief. Go to lunch with them; greet them in a friendly manner—in short, work to disarm them. Ignoring them or being angry with them gives them permission to become an enemy. Remember that there is a part of such people that love a fight—why give them what they want? You might not completely succeed with such individuals but you might take off the edge. A library is not big game for power hunters, so eventually it is likely they will move on and not bother you too frequently after that. The important point in all of this is continually to develop and build your network. The bigger your network, the more power you have and the less vulnerable you are. People think twice about going after well-connected individuals.

Do stay away from the power struggles of others. Obviously, you have to be a close observer of what is occurring. You have to continually read the politics and see who is rising in power. But you should not get caught up in any one else's power struggles because it means that you would have taken sides, and in organizational life you never bet on one horse.

Now given problems like these, some directors think that the price is too high or the effort too troublesome to constantly be engaged in developing a network. If you feel that way, have an honest conversation with yourself. Are you neglecting the development of the political savvy that you need about how organizations work? Are you letting your shyness get the best of you? Are you concerned about your energy level with this constant interaction with others? Are you a bit of hermit and want to be alone more than might be wise in a director's position? If you answered yes to any of this, overcome it. A network is vital for survival no matter how troublesome.

TATTLETALE

Few things are fraught with more danger than talking about others. Most of us feel that we are in a balancing act when we start to gossip. Gossip is a funny thing. On the one hand, we need the vital information that gossip can bring; on the other, we run the risk of what we have said being reported back or used against us.

In spite of this, we cannot be afraid of gossip. Gossip bonds people together because the sharing of confidences requires risk, and risking with another implies trust. The constant exercise of trust builds deeper relationships and a more powerful network.

We also really need the information that gossip brings. I am not talking about engaging in trashing colleagues but knowing the who, what, when, where, and how of people is very important. Through gossip, you receive vital informal communication. The more information you have, the better are your decisions and your actions.

Once in a while, you might hear gossip about something that is criminal, unethical, illegal, or dangerous. Don't hesitate. Report it to your boss. If you think twice about this, as in "I don't want to get involved," then consider the consequences when it is learned that you did know about it, and of course that fact will become known.

More challenging is when you hear something that is just juicy about an individual, which the boss probably would like to know. It is tempting to be the one to share this with the boss so you can enjoy the momentary prestige of being in the know. Inevitably, it gets back to that person that you were the one who told and you will have made an enemy. Creating an enduring enemy for a second of glory is rarely worth it. Generally speaking, keep your eyes wide open but your mouth shut.

Being a tattletale can take another form. Don't become one of those people in organizations that always have a steady stream of ideas as to how other units in the organization could work better. While I am not suggesting that you stifle good ideas, be aware that you are not an expert in the workings of the other unit; there may be cause for things to work the way they do. These criticisms will get back to your peers who at the least will be annoyed and could be very angry. People who are criticized will work to discount their critics; this will rebound and damage your reputation.

Remember your boss isn't taking your steady stream of opinions that well either. Now, you might think you are being an active participant in organizational life. Your boss thinks you are a busybody with time on your hands. This does not apply to any discussions that you might have with your boss about poor services that are provided to your library from other units since there you have a right to expect better. I am only speaking about having continual opinions about how others run their business. Frankly, just mind your own business. You probably aren't running a perfect library. Be always aware that you are in a glass house.

Before you speak, ask yourself if your words will serve your higher purpose of building a strong network.

POACHERS

The more we network, the more we increase the visibility of our libraries. This is a good thing because then our libraries are seen as more powerful. There is however one area in which we could all wish that our libraries had low visibility—and that is, library space.

There is something about libraries that brings out the poachers. So many people want our space. There is a good reason for this: libraries are often large, with appealing spaces, tall ceilings, and a central location. No one seems to be exempt from wanting to poach. Deans of colleges want spaces, city managers want to sell the property, city services want to take over a branch, Friends of the Library want a service relocated so they can have larger space, faculty want offices, teachers want larger teaching or conference spaces, and so forth and so on. The poaching of space never ends.

This chronic problem is now enhanced by the collective awareness of digital resources. People assume that a library no longer needs space. After all, it is all digitized, isn't it? That misconception will continue and will get worse as the digital universe expands.

Since the poaching of space is a problem that will continue, every director needs to continually work on it. We have to continually watch our territory or the library will be filled with services and individuals without any connection to the library at all. Enough of that and the library will have little space for its functions and will be unable to fulfill its mission effectively. Make sure that everyone knows how heavily the library is used. Release the statistics and show the amount of daily traffic. Make sure that every space in the library is occupied and useful for the customers. Never have space unused. Counter the impression that everything is digitized by thoughtful presentations and comments when the opportunity arises. Things are changing, but a library will always need space— it is just that the space will be utilized in different ways and will continually transform to meet the new needs of customers.

If your boss requires you to give up space, consider these points. Push for services that are at least relevant to library service. Do your best to convince your boss of the library's needs and then get over your resentment at what happened if the decision went against you. Push for the services to come under the library's administration. Make agreements with the new tenant about security and other things vital to the library which many units do not understand. In short, make it palatable for you. Always keep in mind that the library space doesn't actually belong to you—it belongs to the parent organization.

Often you have the power to decline a request for space. For example, perhaps the Friends of the Library are seeking a particular space and for solid reasons you decline. However, be ready for the request to come again and again in spite of providing sound reasoning and workable alternatives. Groups can be very persistent in asking for space. As annoying as this gets, it is still better than groups or peers who do an end run around you to your boss. Rather than dealing with you directly, they make an appealing case to your boss. Then you are in the awkward position of defending your space. You might be thoroughly annoyed but go about your response in a thoughtful manner. One tip: avoid at all costs being in a position, such as getting onto a committee, to help the end runner find space. You don't need to be part of the solution unless it protects the library. In fact, you want to keep the library's visibility low when it comes to space discussions. Its profile as a space opportunity is high enough already.

FRIENDS OF THE LIBRARY

Friends of the Library greatly enrich our lives. They give of themselves, their time, and their money to advance our goals. They are a vital part of our network. As with all activities of the library, Friends of the Library must also be managed. Here are a few issues that can occur.

First, the Friends of the Library can begin to wane. Perhaps the membership is shrinking and there is little hope for building it up, or perhaps the membership is aging and no longer has the stamina for big projects and programs. In this case, it is important that you know that sometimes Friends of the Library groups cannot be revitalized. There is always a tendency to think that you can rescue the group. A lot of wasted effort can go into this. This doesn't mean that you shouldn't try to build membership, but there is a point when it just won't work anymore—the interest and resource capacity of neighborhoods and communities change.

In that case, don't be assertive about formally closing the Friends of the Library. This is politically very dangerous for any director because the Friends have a sympathetic image and are usually very well connected politically. Instead, do talk informally with the remaining Friends about the future. They often will realize that the end is inevitable. Part of the reason they will hold on is because it has become a social group—you can assure them that there are ways of still getting together. If you meet with much resistance, just let the group shrink naturally.

Now you might have an active group but they have formed a clique and no one else can join in. This message of exclusion ruins the possibility of new members, who get the cold shoulder when they try to participate. Eventually the Friends will wither if there is no new blood. Sometimes you cannot convince them of the wisdom of adding more people because their agenda—being a small group—is more important to them than being a strong Friends of the Library group. This is another time to let the group shrink naturally. Put no more energy into it.

Luis Herrera: "The one thing every library director should know is that success is all about building relationships. These relationships begin with a genuine respect and caring for the people you work with, fostering strong teams and harnessing their talent to accomplish great things together. Robust relationships allow you to build networks beyond the organization that ultimately help you realize your vision for the library."

Sometimes a Friends of the Library Board is poor at fiscal management. Using money inappropriately, hoarding funds, missing funds, or badly kept records are all of the problems you can encounter. Often you walk right into this when you are a new director. Work with the board to clean up money problems fast even if you face resistance, which you might in the case of Friends who like to hoard money rather than use it for stated purposes of the Friends. Do keep your boss informed. That is not a person who should read about a fiscal problem with the Friends in the newspaper.

I should note that this is one of the main reasons why a director should have an official slot on the Friends Board. If you aren't official, it is very difficult to get access to and control over the funds. Of course, any fiscal problems always put the director in the crosshairs of public opinion regardless.

The other problem is the do-nothing Friends. At some point, it began that the staff started doing too much of the work of the Friends—the programs, the minutes, the agenda, the announcements, and do on. Never start down that path, and if you inherited it, start to wean the Friends away. You will shortly find out if you have a true Friends group or just a social club.

COMMUNITY GROUPS

As part of your effort to build a strong network, become an active participant in community groups. Organizations such as Kiwanis, Rotary, Lions, or Chambers of Commerce as examples are all excellent groups that you can join. What a great way to meet movers and shakers including business owners, judges, developers, the editor and publisher of your local paper, medical and legal professionals, and more.

Connie Vinita Dowell: "When I started out, I wish I had known that my main purpose was communication and translation not only above and below me on the organizational chart but to all areas of the university and the external community."

Of course, be strategic. Don't waste your time on a small group but instead join the group that is the largest and most the active. Then take on visible tasks, join high-profile committees, and hold office. Become known as someone who can be counted on. You know the old saying "see and be seen." In time, you will come to know and be known literally by hundreds of people.

Heads up for those of you starting out joining a community organization: Not only will the organization have dues, luncheons, and fund-raisers but you will also get requests from other members to support their causes. Everyone has an agenda for being in that organization in addition to the mission of the organization. Rarely does a library have a budget that allows these kinds of costs. Therefore, it is a personal expense and a question for your tax accountant. Budget yourself, or your costs can go sky high. Don't succumb to pressure because many of these clubs have the pace set by some high rollers who can afford to spend freely—usually way out of the financial league of a library director.

Never forget the natural allies of libraries such as historical associations, book clubs, writers' associations, and museums. And always know your other librarian neighbors. Sometimes as librarians we travel too much with like librarians. For example, if you are a university librarian, get to know the public librarian down the block. If you are a public librarian, meet the community college librarian. Cast your net far and wide.

I do want to note that sometimes historical associations, made up largely of dedicated volunteers, can be wary of libraries. There is a belief that we want their resources. While privately you might believe that some of their resources would be better managed in a library setting, you have to reassure them that is not your intent. Form a network with them to advance the cause of local history. They will appreciate the attention and you will have gained good friends.

STUDENT ASSOCIATIONS

In any college or school setting, there are many varieties of student associations including the student government, specialty clubs such as science or language, cultural affiliations, athletic groups, honor societies, or sororities and fraternities. It is important to have cordial relationships with them all, but realistically you can only focus on a few because of the time involved for you and your staff. Therefore, you need be strategic about building your network with student associations.

Working closely and effectively with the student government is the most important action you can take. Here are some best practices: take the president and vice-president to lunch, first when they are elected, and then with a couple of follow-up lunches throughout the year; make sure they have your contact information and make sure that the staff who answers the phone know who they are so they have rapid access to you; encourage them to speak with you directly on any student concerns; attend the inauguration of student officers; and attend their annual awards banquet. The students will really appreciate your active and visible support. Of course, you don't have to do this all yourself—other managers and staff should be visible too. While year after year may go by without any incident concerning students, when there is an issue, you will have established a solid foundation.

Do request to be included on the agenda of the student senate a couple of times a year, so that you can update the student senators on emerging issues, new projects, or programs. Seek their input. This is mutually beneficial. They will appreciate being asked and being in the know early. You will get some good ideas. If ideas for joint projects between student government and the library come up, make every effort to approve these ideas.

> ***Penny Markey***: "Every director should encourage the care and feeding of their children and young adult services staff. They should recognize the inherent importance of the work that they do in creating a library presence in the community. Even if parents and caregivers don't acknowledge the value of library services for themselves—they certainly view them as valuable for their children."

Always invite the presidents and members of student government, clubs, and societies to every event. When you have a dedication or major event, the president of student government should be invited to speak. Now once in a while, a student government president will make a public remark that might be embarrassing for or critical of the college or school or worse, the library. Usually this is an attempt to be funny but not always. Just sit there graciously and mentally move on. Don't forget that you are likely on camera so no visible reaction is best. Rarely can an inappropriate public remark be deflected on the spot unless you are up next to speak, are naturally quick on your feet, and very witty. You don't want to make the situation worse.

Do look for every opportunity to reach out to all student associations. This might include library participation in such events as clubs and activities fairs, hosting student events within the library, and providing space in the library for student clubs and associations.

As part of this effort, make sure that the library is active in outreach to potential students who are as yet unaffiliated with any student association. The best way is by participating in an orientation for freshmen and transfers. Another mode of outreach is to provide tours for potential students and parents. You can't start early enough in establishing the library's positive relationship with students.

Fairly often, student associations organize protests for various causes. Since libraries are usually well located with wide entrances and appealing spaces, they are often the site of student protests. When a protest occurs, always keep in mind that you and your staff want to maintain the most cordial of relationships to students. You and your staff should stand back and let the students march and chant in and around your library. You don't want any actions from the library's staff to be the spark that lights a fire under the protestors.

Of course, sometimes protestors will start vandalizing or stealing or become violent toward staff and customers. Unruly protests are the business of campus administration and campus police—who hopefully have policies and procedures in place for such a contingency. Your library's emergency handbook should have clear directions for your staff on how to secure the most valuable library assets. Of course, your staff should know that you consider them to be the most valuable of all. While you might applaud the bravery and commitment of staff in protecting the library's resources and equipment, you do not want any human being harmed in the process.

Now of course, if the library is the reason for the protests, you will need to meet with the student leaders and see if you can get a resolution. This is another reason for you to have already laid the groundwork of friendship with student leaders. You won't be negotiating with strangers. Regardless, never go alone to such meetings, though; have the dean of students with you. Most clubs and associations have a faculty or staff liaison, so if such groups are the source of the protests, invite the liaison to join you too. Do make sure that you are keeping your boss in the loop in order for him or her to guide and support you. Additionally, if the protestors want something that is unreasonable and you cannot find a resolution, you will have to refer it to your boss, so it is best that the boss has a full understanding of the issue early.

Sometimes, around exam time especially, student groups will organize flash mobs, undie runs, and so forth—much of which now ends up on YouTube. Don't take any action and don't worry about it. Much of it is just young people letting off steam, enjoying being nonconformists, and just having fun. Also, if you do protest or try to restrain their actions, you and your library will be on YouTube and not in a good way. One negative video there will destroy a year of good networking.

ELECTED OFFICIALS

No matter what type of library you are in, it is a good idea to pay attention to all elected officials such as members of congress or senators. In addition to the impact that legislation can have on libraries, elected officials have considerable sway over resources and special funds—some of which could benefit your library. Always keep in contact with elected officials or, more usually with their legislative aides. Visit once a year to keep them informed about broader library issues and contact them throughout the year if you have relevant information for anything coming up involving libraries. Make yourself known as someone who has sound facts about libraries, intellectual property, or literacy issues. Remember they are building their network too and might have need of a person with expert information. Naturally, you will always work in the context of the parent organization's legislative agenda so you don't accidentally provide a contrary argument or fuel to defeat your parent organization's legislative goals.

Keep your eye out for the possibility of being appointed to a commission or a neighborhood committee. Thus you will increase your profile, and therefore your power, while making a contribution and meeting interesting people too.

It may occur that you have to present before a legislative hearing on libraries or related matters as an expert. Make your comments short, pithy, and quotable. Do vet your remarks with colleagues or with media experts so you will not say something that could be accidentally misunderstood. Otherwise, relate to the legislators as you would to any board.

CONCLUSION

All of this networking requires stamina in a busy day. You may want to faint with the thought of one more chicken and rice dinner, hearing one story that you have heard a dozen times, or listening to points of view and political opinions with which you deeply disagree. You do it for the library—to build its network continually. Fortunately, many supporters with whom you are networking are engaging, charming, and full of interesting stories; their company is a pleasure.

One final and important point: building a network is not something you do once and then don't bother again. You must always be building your network and making important connections between people. It takes a lot of energy, but there are few actions that pay off as well as a strong network.

For more writings by me on this subject, see "Positioning the Library," *College and University Libraries Journal,* Vol. 4, No. 2, November, 1997.

Chapter Seven

Dealing with the Press

Being the chief spokesperson for the library is one of the many jobs that come with being a library director. Sooner or later you must deal with the press. Now, there are many dimensions to dealing with the press, including being interviewed one-on-one with media of any kind including appearing on TV, sending out news releases, holding media events, and of course managing the fast breaking-world of social media.

Regardless of the mode of dealing with the press, being successful in getting our message across in a manner that is both compelling and accurate requires considerable thought and planning. Let's look now at what every library director should know about dealing with the press.

THE DOUBLE-EDGED SWORD

I want to acknowledge up front that dealing with the press is a double-edged sword. On the one hand, getting positive press for the library, its events, its new services, or its achievements is enjoyable and rewarding. On the other hand, if something has gone wrong, getting negative press can be a horrible experience.

Many of us starting out in our careers as directors are often delighted to see our names in the paper. We send the clipping or link to our friends and family and put it into our own memory files. Toward the end of our careers however, after seeing for years the double-edged sword of the press toward ourselves and others, most of us never want to be called by a reporter again.

You might not get over that feeling, but we do have to get our ego out of the way, because dealing with the press is an important part of the job. Getting press coverage is still one of the best ways to get the message out about the library. Pleasure and pain are part of dealing with the press, so treat these feelings both the same with the cool professionalism that is your heritage.

BEING INTERVIEWED: PREPARATION

Being interviewed is the most stressful of all the activities dealing with the press. It is an area of considerable challenge because the director is being called upon to speak spontaneously and knowledgeably while under the pressure of making sure that every word is right and will not be misinterpreted.

Preparation is the key to success here. Generally speaking, unless you have a fast breaking issue, there is usually some time to prepare for an interview. You know when the interview is going to take place and you know what it is about and you know who is going to interview you.

Begin by anticipating the questions and rehearsing the answers. However, don't just focus on the subject of the interview. Do think about anything else the reporter might ask, especially if there have been any problems lately.

Write out the message that you want to get across because you will repeat those themes throughout the interview. Writing it out helps you to clarify it and also to remember it. Don't have more than one or two messages. More than a couple of messages gets confusing for the listener, and you run the risk of not remembering more than two when you are under pressure.

Be ready with sound bites—those catchy phrases which make good headlines and quotes. In fact, whenever you think of a sound bite, even if you are not being interviewed, write it down and keep it in your press file.

Do keep a continuing press file in which you have interesting facts and figures, compelling stories, or unusual events. This file is very useful in preparing for an interview and also in giving an interview on the phone or the radio where looking through a file is not seen. It helps to jog your memory.

Be very careful not to use library speak. Those aren't stacks, but shelves. Those aren't our holdings, but the collection. Those aren't users, but customers or students. Watch out for the acronyms too, as they can confound the uninitiated.

You don't have to interview by yourself. If you have access to a public relations specialist, invite that person to be at the interview with you. In fact, ask him or her to review your message, your sound bites, as well as the potential questions and answers you have prepared.

Now sometimes the interview subject might require a colleague who has expertise in the topic. For example, perhaps the interview is about a rare collection in your library and the curator is the best person to provide detail. Do review together the message, potential questions and answers, and any issues that might come up. Make sure that you have complete confidence in that individual to handle the press. Sometimes people love to hear the sound of their own voice.

Now once in a while, you may have to respond to legal issues. Generally speaking, this should be avoided at all costs but if you do have to, then make sure that your attorney has reviewed all of your materials. Better yet, have the attorney with you or have the attorney speak for you.

Think about the backdrop of the interview. What is the scenery behind you? Often interviews are accompanied by pictures, so you want to think about that in advance. What is the message that you want to convey through the backdrop? Fortunately most libraries have some beautiful spaces for an interview—handsome shelving, children's areas, or nice lounges, so there are a lot of good choices. Do be mindful of interviews in your office. Family photos, joke objects, and so on that you don't want the general public to see should all be tucked away.

Make sure that your interview is in a private space. You don't want to have an unintended audience. You don't want to find yourself on YouTube. Now sometimes you might want to be interviewed in a public space—just be mindful of what you are doing and what the risks are. One risk obviously is that the reporter may wander around and ask the customers what they think of this or that issue. These unscripted moments can become a public relations nightmare.

Remember that different media call for different approaches. Think about it in advance. Match your tone, your body language, and your clothing to the occasion. If you are giving bad or tragic news, that is no time for bright colors, lively ties, heavy jewelry, and big smiles. However, at all times, good eye contact and warmth of voice are appropriate.

If you are going to be on camera, prepare yourself with this important point. When you finish your response or when the reporter is asking a question, relax your face and have no expression on it. Never forget that the camera is always on you. Sometimes we give away what we are really feeling in those moments between speaking. That is not a time to show that you are critical, sarcastic, disgusted, or irritated. Keep your face neutral. People will remember your expression; any wrong expression will defeat what you have to say.

THE WRITTEN WORD

If you are preparing for an interview or a media event, developing a public relations packet is a good idea. It should contain information pertaining to the subject as well as a description of the library, its most interesting features, and its most compelling statistics. Even if your website is extensive, reporters do appreciate that they don't have to do any digging.

Regarding your website, do consider having a section that can be used routinely by the press for background information. The library's history and timeline, important facts, some quotes by you, interesting photos, awards, and selected services of the library can all be featured. Consider also links to important sites such as ALA for issues such as intellectual freedom. Maintaining web pages for the press means you don't have to keep recreating the information that not only saves time but also increases accuracy since the information won't be created in a hurry.

But whether you are having a public relations packet created, issuing a news release, or blogging about an upcoming event, make sure that the written word is thoroughly proofread. It does seem so obvious, but how often have you seen errors in information, or broken links, or embarrassing spelling mistakes?

Now sometimes the information might be going out about a culture or language that is not your own. Make sure that whatever is written is reviewed by someone who is familiar with that culture or language. It is very easy to offend when we don't fully understand a culture or language.

The bottom line is that you are responsible for information that goes out about the library. Make sure you are the final reviewer. Any errors or inaccuracies will belong to you once it goes out so make every effort to get it correct.

BEING INTERVIEWED: RESPONDING

Now comes the tough part—your responses to the reporter's questions. Let me say this up front—you don't have to answer every question that is put to you. If you get a question that you don't want to answer, answer instead with what you want to say. It is a rare reporter that will challenge you on that. Stay on your message.

One of the tough things about being a librarian is that we are deeply programmed to respond to questions. Those years of making sure that our customers get the answers they need have shaped us. We also can be too literal and therefore too concerned about answering exactly. Don't get so lost in answering questions automatically or precisely that you forget that an interview is essentially a political process. Just don't let your librarian programming kick in.

Watch out for the questions that don't seem to be questions. Sometimes reporters just start to chat at the beginning or end of an interview in order to draw you in. Don't chat back but instead stay silent with an interested look on your face unless you are exchanging the mildest of pleasantries. This brings us to an important point—there is no such thing as off the record. It doesn't matter what the reporter says; let me repeat, there is no such thing as off the record.

Do pause before you answer. Listen to the question carefully. Don't pause so long that you look like you are up to something or are fishing for an answer but don't jump the gun. Give yourself a second to think. The brain works very fast under pressure and a moment helps it a lot.

Always be positive. Remember that you are influencing public attitudes. If the reporter asks you something in a negative way, never repeat that negative statement because then you own it. Instead focus on setting the record straight.

Make sure your answers are only a few seconds long no matter what medium the interview is in. You risk the reporter and your audience losing interest and being cut off before you get to your point. Even if you are in a setting where more detail is called for, still be economical in your responses. Get your point across early and fast.

If the reporter is taking notes, speak slowly enough and with enough pauses so that they can catch up with their notes. You don't want them filling in the blanks for you. You can ask the reporter if you can review the interview before it goes public. It rarely happens, but it is worth asking.

If they ask you something you don't know it is okay to say so, but don't leave that comment hanging there. Instead, return to your own agenda by a comment such as, "As I mentioned earlier . . ." Stay on your message and don't get distracted.

Now once in a while we realize that we have misspoken in the interview. Take a lesson from the Olympians—when they fall, they get up and keep on going. If you have misspoken, correct yourself immediately but don't let your mind dwell on it throughout the interview because a distracted mind will impact the quality of the rest of your responses. Additionally, your body language will show that you are distracted.

Here are some other basics: don't joke, because jokes aren't always understood the way you intended them; never volunteer information, because that could open up a road you don't want to go on; never get hostile, angry, or defensive no matter what they ask, because you will find that your anger gets the headlines and increases a reporter's natural suspicion; never be afraid to apologize if the library has created a customer service problem; and never get unnerved by a reporter who asks the same question several times but instead realize that they are digging for a story.

Let me just say, never forget when the microphone is on. A year does not go by that a famous person or a public speaker has forgotten a hot microphone and says something that was never intended for the public. We all get a laugh about those moments but not if it is us. Say nothing and make no comments until you are back in the privacy of your own office.

Do recap to your boss immediately after an interview. This is one person that should never be taken by surprise. Also, if the parent organization has a public relations department, copy them too. They will appreciate it.

Do read or watch or listen to whatever has been written or shown even if you are horrified by the result. This is an arena in which you are always learning.

THE DROP-IN REPORTER

More often than not the reporter will "drop-in" by making a phone call but sometimes in person. There are two good reasons a reporter has for doing this. A reporter is always on deadline and really doesn't have the time to be making appointments on fast-breaking issues. Additionally, every reporter knows the value of the element of surprise. He or she wants the spontaneous response and the unguarded moment.

Now what happens with the drop-in reporter on the phone or in person? Just know that you don't have to be interviewed if you are not ready or don't want to talk about the subject. It is easy to decline—just don't be available. Hopefully you have a secretary or office staff that is trained in being an excellent filter for you. They know how to find out who is asking for you and what is wanted. As part of that training, give them precise phrases to say such as "I am sorry but the director is not available at this time. May I take a message?" Otherwise, you run the risk of staff making up a response on the spot such as "I am sorry the director is not available although I did just see her/him a moment ago." Advise them to give out as little information as possible; otherwise, they might end up being interviewed themselves.

Now if the reporter catches you in the public area then be gracious but never cornered. You just don't have to be interviewed right then if you don't want to be. Reschedule for another time, let the reporter know you will call, or ask him or her to email you the questions—the latter rarely works but it is worth a shot.

Now sometimes we get calls from reporters who want to get our reaction about an issue related to the parent organization, to a breaking news story, or to an occurrence in a nearby library. If you aren't the right spokesperson for the issue, then just decline and refer the reporter to someone who is. Again it is better to have your secretary find out why the reporter is calling. Then if you don't want to make any comments, your secretary can call back the reporter to decline on your behalf. That way, you don't get accidentally drawn into an interview you don't want to have.

> ***Brian E. C. Schottlaender:*** "The one thing that every library director should know is that perception **IS.** What people hear, see, and feel is what shapes their view of reality, and no amount of your telling them that reality is different is going to change that. So, take a leaf from Aldous Huxley and focus as much of your attention on perception as you do on reality. Or more."

THE REPORTER: FRIEND OR FOE?

I think that we all have a complex relationship with reporters. On the one hand, there is deep appreciation that they work hard to support a free and open society. They bring issues to public attention and their work changes lives and society for the better. Sometimes they even die in the course of a story. On the other hand, none of us want to be under their microscope.

To give an effective interview, do read the newspapers or the relevant blogs and social media regularly. Do get to know who the reporters are and how they usually write. Are they a reporter who does exposés or do they cover the fun and charming events around town? When you hear that this reporter wants to talk to you, if you know the person already, you can anticipate the story angle.

Remember that no reporter is a friend. Reporters love libraries but not at the expense of their own careers. If they smell a story, they will track it down. Sometimes this is complicated by the fact that you might know a reporter personally who could even be in your social circle. Difficult as this is, always remember that you have a reporter in your midst.

Be conscious of the fact that reporters are skilled in certain interview techniques. The same way that we know how to conduct the reference interview is the same way that they know how to conduct the one-on-one interview. They can appear sympathetic to draw you in. They could surprise you with information perhaps by even quoting someone else, such as a staff member, on the subject. They might fire several questions at once at you or finish your sentences for you. Just don't get riled up—keep to your message and keep the record accurate.

Now sometimes a reporter really does a bad job and reports very inaccurately. First, let your boss, the public relations department if you have one, and your staff know that the report is inaccurate. You definitely don't want people this important to you thinking that the story was correct. Very quickly, that is, that day, you will have to correct the information and get your side of the story out to the general public. Certainly you have a right to expect that a correction will be issued and your letter to the editor published. You could request another interview, but it rarely happens and you face the risk of dealing with that reporter again. Don't forget about providing the correct information on the library's website and social media. You can't just let the story sit there. People still believe what they read even if they say they don't. Bad information still influences us.

Then of course there is the student reporter working for a college paper. Some of these students are excellent and some are not cut out for the job. You might find something about your library reported inaccurately or yourself seriously misquoted. Take the same actions listed above but if the problem continues, you also may wish to speak with the advisor to the college newspaper, who is often a faculty member. While many college newspapers are deemed independent, sometimes the advisor can influence the situation directly or indirectly. Even if you get frustrated, always keep in mind that these are students and they are learning the job.

Some reporters can get very aggressive, especially those who want to make a name for themselves as investigative reporters. They might get very pushy. Don't lose your patience or your temper. Don't make yourself the story.

BAD PRESS DAY

Let's talk about bad press resulting from a problem that has occurred within the library. Bad press can come from a wide variety of issues, for example, an unhappy customer, large fiscal errors, censorship, serious accidents in the library, physical fights between customers, unchecked graffiti, gang turf wars, a technology failure, or a large homeless population in the reading rooms. A reporter can turn any of these issues into bad press for the library.

Again, you want to get on this fast because you can't let bad press be the last word on your library even though the reporting of the problem is legitimate. Get the full story out so that readers have a more complete understanding of the problem and its challenges. Do explain what you are already doing to correct the situation. Do apologize where you need to apologize. Do point out collaborations with other agencies such as police or social services that are helping you to rectify the problem. In other words, make the story fact-based and rational—this will help to reduce sensationalism—which is so much the hallmark of the press. Of course if there is a possibility of a lawsuit relating to this problem, speak with your attorney before releasing a statement.

Now sometimes, the reporter does not stop there but goes after you as the head of the library and the person ultimately responsible for its management. This can be very painful. It also creates fear for your own future, for your reputation, and for your effectiveness. At the very least, it is an embarrassing situation. Take a deep breath. Don't get scared: let no event be bigger than you. Stay the course, and again keep all your responses fact-based and rational. No matter how hurtful the reporter's words are, don't let anger or hurt or anxiety color your response. It will only make it worse, and you might start sounding like you are a problem. Keep in mind that you are not alone: you aren't the first and won't be the last director caught in the crosshairs of the press.

You and your staff should scour the press of all kinds every day and keep tabs on what is said about your library. You really don't want to be the last to know or be caught by surprise by a reporter calling to get more detail. Naturally, you will keep key people, like your boss or the board, in the loop at all times. If it is bad enough, they will be dragged in anyway and you will want them to be prepared with your side of the story.

TWO WEEK RULE

I have observed throughout my career that most crises reported in the press last about two weeks. After that, other events occur and the public interest moves on. Working in any press job is very fast moving, so no reporter can afford to linger, be behind the times, and focus on stale news.

When you have a public relations disaster, consider my theory that bad press has an arc of about two weeks. Even though you might want to head for the hills for six months, you can bear two weeks. However, do be aware that if the situation is a big problem then the reporter, on a slow day, will cycle back to you. Therefore, keep cleaning up the problem so that if the news story cycles back, you can report that is it solved or well underway to being solved.

STAFF INVOLVEMENT

Do have a media policy in place. In all likelihood, the parent organization, if you have one, already has a policy, but the library should have its own too. The policy should cover basics so that staff know who is authorized to speak for the library, what actions to take when a reporter calls, how to report if they have responded to a reporter's question, and so forth. As part of that media policy, make sure your staff knows that they have to report immediately to you when a reporter is in the building. The wandering reporter who just pops in looking for a quote, and catches people unawares, can be a problem.

As a director, you really don't want all and everyone speaking on a library issue, and if this does occur, you need to make sure that you know exactly what happened and exactly what was said. If everyone feels free to comment on anything regardless of their expertise or awareness then you will have a confused public message going out, and if the issue is serious enough, you may be spending some time in damage control.

In some settings, such as a corporate or armed forces library, it is easier to have a policy that only certain people speak to the press. In a university, with its liberal traditions, it is almost impossible to govern that. However, most staff would rather avoid being in the news and only deal with reporters if they absolutely have to. Now, there are staff, driven by their egos or by mischief, who are eager to get their quote in.

Let's talk about the employee with the big ego for a moment. Sometimes an employee just wants to be the one quoted in the press, the one whose picture is there, the go-to-person for the press. This is the person that talks to the press and doesn't report to you or lets you know much later that a reporter was in the building. It is likely they will also be the one who is writing to the press too. This is truly a problem because they are such a wild card. The person's supervisor has to sit down with this employee and review with them the media policy and why it exists. If the employee has created a mess by giving inaccurate or negative information to the press, make sure he or she knows about it and what damage has been done. Make sure the employee knows the effort involved in cleaning up the problem. It might make the employee think twice next time a reporter comes calling because a big ego does not care for embarrassment. However, big egos are tough to manage. Additionally, disciplinary action can be very difficult here as a director can wander easily into the domain of free speech.

Now ordinarily, no one should release anything formally about the library without your review and approval. However, in social media, such as Twitter, you obviously can't review every feed. Therefore, do develop a team of staff skilled in social media to help market the library. However, be aware that whatever they write is your responsibility. Therefore, give them the training that they need. You cannot expect staff starting out to have the same political savvy that you have developed over the years. Of course, be careful who is initially on the social media team—common sense is the desirable ingredient.

You don't always have to be the one giving the interviews, so do provide the training that is needed. In terms of a succession plan, this is good experience for anyone who shows promise in becoming a director. You will find that there are some staff that are superb at giving interviews. They are just naturals at this. If so, when certain issues arise that falls within their expertise, give them a chance to be interviewed.

CONCLUSION

Even though dealing with the press is not a daily event, it still calls for continual on-the-job training. Read all you can about press relations, attend workshops whenever there is an opportunity, and be a student of dealing with the press in all its forms. You can never be too prepared.

Develop your own nose for the news. As a director you have to be alert to what is newsworthy whether or not it is positive or negative for the library. Get on issues fast. You want to be the one managing the situation.

When it comes to the press, you have to have your wits about you. The press is not our domain, so it calls for us to think things through carefully. We have to be very alert, because once something is in the press it is there forever and the image of our library is at stake.

Chapter Eight

A Death in the Library

What can be a sadder event in a library than the passing of a colleague? The loss of one of our own is a devastating event. There are very few libraries that have not experienced the passing of a colleague, but there is almost nothing written about what a director should do. Is there really a management process surrounding death? Yes, there is, and it is important for every library director to know what steps to take and what will be encountered in managing a death in the library.

If ever there was a time for leadership this is it. Your staff needs you and will look to you to do all the right things. This chapter is about doing the right things even though you may be called upon to believe the unbelievable and accept the unacceptable.

EMOTIONAL IMPACT

First of all, the emotional impact will vary from staff member to staff member. Not all staff will feel sad the same way. Likely, everyone will have a degree of sadness, but "degree" is the important word here. Staff will range along a spectrum of emotions from those who are simply sorry to hear about the passing of a colleague to those who are devastated by the loss. Cruelly, there may even be one or two who are glad your late colleague is gone. Your task is to know which members of your staff are experiencing the greatest emotional impact because you will need to be particularly attentive to those who are the saddest.

Being attentive to those who are saddest is complicated by scale if many are grieving. This particularly occurs when a long-term, beloved colleague passes. I add the word "beloved" because there are long-term colleagues who pass but who have never managed to work their way into the hearts of colleagues. When most of your staff are grieving, don't be surprised at an eerie silence across the library for several days as you and your staff collectively process grief. The only exception will be the sounds related to direct customer service, but even those tones will be hushed and respectful. Just let the grief flow in the time and the manner needed. A little later in this chapter, we will talk about the difficult business of doing business during this time.

The manner of the passing also changes the emotional impact. A person whose death is anticipated through long illness does not have the shock of a person dying suddenly. In the former, there is some degree of mental preparation, in the latter, none at all.

The cause of death also changes the emotional impact. If a staff member dies from substance abuse, carelessness about health, or risky behavior, there can be residual anger, mixed with sadness, by the staff at the deceased. Staff can be angry that their late colleague didn't take the right steps to preserve life.

Suicide, so sad anyway, can sometimes create collective guilt because perhaps there was something that could have been done, that should have been seen. Everyone might be asking, "Did we fail to read the signs?" However, none of you were to know—you are library workplace colleagues, not therapists. Do be aware that staff may become angry at the late colleague's supervisor, or management in general, as the workplace is sometimes seen unfairly as a reason for the suicide. Be prepared for the backlash of anger no matter how unfair.

Now perhaps there was a disciplinary action underway. Your late colleague could have been a problem employee. While the staff may have been angry at their late colleague over poor performance or behavior while alive, they sometimes then turn that anger toward you and any other supervisor. It is as if they feel guilt over their own anger, worry that it contributed to the suicide, and then find relief from this guilt by blaming management. Don't internalize this guilt—you had to take actions that you had to take relating to a problem employee. And above all, don't let this tragedy prevent you from taking future action on problems.

Allow people their anger. Ease the anger and correct the misconceptions where you can by compassionate language and understanding. These angry feelings will pass. Do be mindful though that sometimes there is a covertly hostile employee who sees an opportunity to spread a hurtful rumor that management's actions directly caused the death of the late colleague. Even the presence of death does not inhibit some people.

Do be prepared for the emotional response if your late colleague had relatives on the staff. A spouse, children, in-laws, cousins, or parents might also work for your library. This is a double blow of sadness as your staff will feel sad not only for your late colleague but also for the family member or members whom they know and work with.

Let's talk for a moment about your own emotions. You will be along a spectrum too—you could be stunned by grief at the passing of a close colleague or simply sad that someone on your staff has died. Be careful not to fabricate more than you feel. You have to be honest in your own emotions and not gush with sadness because you think that is expected of you. No one will believe you anyway—people are not fooled—and you will damage your own credibility. If you are not devastated, then you are not. Just maintain your usual respectful approach.

The greatest challenge for directors is to hold their own emotions in check. No matter how sad you are, you have to take your library through this grief. You have a library full of grieving people who will look to you at this time. This doesn't mean that you have to be stoic but you cannot be indulgent with yourself either and give way to your emotions. You have a job to do. By the way, don't be surprised if no one cares how you feel. It is a rare staff member who actually will ask you how you are doing. Somehow employees don't expect you to have these emotions or they are simply too self-absorbed with their own grief at this time.

THE DYING COLLEAGUE

Often a person is hospitalized and/or in hospice care for some time before passing. If your colleague or the family (if your colleague is unable to communicate) wants it, then naturally you will inform the staff of this sad situation. People vary greatly in their needs for privacy but some may want visitors, flowers, cards, and so on. Some of your staff will want to go and make their goodbyes. As hard as this is, you also need to go, assuming that you are on good terms with your colleague. What do you say to a dying colleague? Always you have to take his or her lead. Some people who are passing want to talk about it and want to say goodbye; some don't. Some may be in complete denial. But if appropriate, recall a sweet memory that you shared. Say thanks for the years of contribution. I would say, "It has been an honor to be your friend and colleague."

One of the most heart-wrenching conversations you will ever have is when a colleague comes to tell you about a terminal diagnosis. In addition to your words of compassion and encouragement, ask your colleague how you can help, what he or she needs at this time, and how can the staff offer support. Usually your colleague will have a purpose in addition to letting you know. He or she may want to inform you of intent to retire early, to resign, to go on extended sick leave, to go half-time, or to work for just a little while longer. Your colleague might request a move to lighter duties. Help where you can help and accommodate where you can accommodate.

Occasionally, your colleague will ask you to keep the diagnosis confidential. You can agree to this up to a point. Obviously, your colleague's supervisor, your library's personnel manager, and your other top level managers need to know. You cannot have such a serious matter occurring in the library without these managers knowing.

Now sometimes your colleague will want to keep on with the job as before and work to the very end. Sometimes the employee is in denial, wants to hang on to something solid in his or her disappearing world, wants to be distracted from the awful reality, wants to continue to make a meaningful contribution, or wants some combination of all. The challenge for you and the rest of your staff is that a critically ill employee can rarely do the job at the level that is needed—there will be missing days and a waning of energy and of the ability to concentrate. The work will gradually be seriously impacted. Organizationally, the needs of the overall library take precedence over the needs of an individual. However, in a sad situation such as this, the needs of both are aligned. You are maintaining your values of respect and compassion while enabling a colleague to face the end with dignity. Many times you and your staff can simply adjust. Staff are very willing to help out at this time. You can recruit them or they will often volunteer to take on part of the portfolio of work in order to get the job done.

Now once in a while a critically ill colleague resists this assistance because it is an overt acknowledgement of what is to come. A conversation with your colleague will be called for even though you will dislike troubling a colleague who is facing eternity with work matters.

This conversation will be naturally very supportive and will center on the need of your colleague to focus on health while still enabling the library to move the work forward. Be prepared for a range of reactions from upset and anger ("I'm not dead yet!") to sadness over yet one more loss to relief. Fortunately most people do know when they cannot do the entire job anymore so they will appreciate the help, the relief, and the respect. And usually, if there is any anger or upset about another having to do part of the work, it usually is at the circumstance not at fellow colleagues.

DYING IN THE LIBRARY

Sometimes a colleague dies in the workplace witnessed by fellow colleagues. The horror of the catastrophic event, the arrival of emergency services, the desperate attempt to rescue, and the stunned aftermath is so traumatic.

Then, of course, the family must be told, and that is the most awful duty in the world. The first decision is who calls. Sometimes it is the police, sometimes an assistant coroner, sometimes a police chaplain, sometimes you, sometimes a staff member who was close to your late colleague, as examples. While you hope that so sad an occasion never occurs, you should know the policy of your parent organization or local jurisdiction about who calls. If you are in a stand-alone library, then it should be written into your policy.

The next decision is how to contact the next of kin. If close, a visit is best however awful. If far away, the decision to phone is made for you. Obviously, it is vital that every library have an up-to-date next of kin list with contact information. Make sure that you and key managers and supervisors also have that information available if you are at home: this is where a password controlled library intranet is so useful. By the way, don't rely on the parent organization's human resources department to provide you with the next of kin. Most libraries are open on weekends and evenings; human resources is not.

Do be prepared for this saddest of news to get out before the formal notification of next of kin. There is always someone who wants to jump on social media and be the first to report a death in the library. Additionally, there are people who habitually listen to police scanners and may also get right onto social media also.

Sometimes the family will contact you later to understand in more detail what happened. If you or whoever on your staff witnessed your colleague's passing, it is a decent thing to tell the family what they need to know. In particular, families are always interested in the possibility of final words that may be messages. Our last moments on earth are precious to those who love us best.

Now it might be that the death was caused by an accident in the workplace. A fall from a ladder, a slip down the stairs, a blow by loose piece of equipment stored overhead, a road accident in the bookmobile, and more are all possibilities in our libraries. In this case, if it is likely that the library or the parent organization might be at fault or be sued regardless, you might not be able to comment on anything at all. At that point, the attorneys take over. Not being able to comment is very hard, but keep in mind that it can occur.

I have not discussed what you should do when a violent or suspicious death of a colleague occurs in the workplace. Your policies and procedures regarding this horrifying event should be clearly laid out in your emergency plan. Every worst-case scenario should be covered in your plan, and of course your staff must be completely familiar with it.

There is one point that I want to mention about emergency plans related to violent or suspicious deaths. If the situation allows, remember how important it is for you to allow no one, other than emergency personnel, into the area of the scene of death. This area must be secure in case a crime has occurred. You should also require everyone to stay on site as witnesses and, sadly, as possible suspects. Do make sure that you secure the video from your security cameras so you can hand it over to the police: it might contain vital evidence. The police will be on site shortly and take it from there, but they only have one chance to get it right, so do your brief but important part to preserve evidence and retain witnesses.

SHARING THE NEWS

You are the voice of the library, and it is your responsibility to inform every one of the passing of your colleague. Let's look first at how you will inform the staff.

There will be several stages of sharing. As soon as you can, and assuming they are not witnesses to the passing, reach the people most affected by your colleague's passing. Go directly to their work areas and see them in person. People will appreciate hearing it in person and as soon as possible. Ask them if they want to take some time off, go for a walk, have a long lunch, or a coffee with each other—they need time, physically and mentally, to absorb the blow. They will very much appreciate your consideration.

If your colleague passes on the weekend, call staff who you know were your late colleague's close friends and allies. If there are many people that you have to reach, then ask other managers or supervisors to help you—in short, activate that good old-fashioned phone tree. Do know that you will not reach everyone partly because of their availability but also because you don't know everyone who is close to the individual. You will kick yourself that you forgot someone that you should have thought of, but remember that you are under pressure too and doing the best you can.

Next, get an email out to let the entire staff know so that they are among the first to hear. News about a colleague passing travels quickly, and you don't want your staff to hear the news from someone, for example, in another unit. This should be a short, respectful message, with the comment that you will send out a fuller message later.

Then, when you have time to compose it properly, send a message that is a tribute to the person and covers his or her background and contribution and describes what this sad loss has meant to you all. In both of these messages, be aware that your message will go far and wide beyond the library. Craft it carefully and make sure that someone else reviews it before it goes out so that there are no comments that could be taken in the wrong way or no information that is inaccurate.

Be sure to let your boss know as soon as possible as well as the human resources department. You should make contact with your boss, but another staff member, usually the one who handles personnel matters, should reach human resources. Your boss should handle any public announcements to the parent organization, but be prepared that your boss may incorporate or simply forward your message.

Don't forget about the professional or community associations with whom your late colleague was involved. They need to know too. Eventually, you can send to the professional journals a photo and new release so that the wider community of librarians is aware. Save everything that is published to send to the family as a tender memento.

Do let the staff participate in getting the word out. They want to do all they can, so be clear in your message that anyone can forward your message. Again, you don't know everyone that your late colleague knew, but the staff together can reach most everyone. Let the staff post your entire message or a truncated form to social media, listservs, or any other mode.

Also, don't forget to inform retirees and other former employees who knew the person. They will appreciate it.

Of course, at this time, you will not know funeral arrangements. Therefore, do note in your formal message that you will let everyone know when you hear from the family. As soon as you hear, let your staff know even if there is no funeral or it is private or it is too remote to attend. People really appreciate knowing what is happening regardless. Once in a while you simply never hear of any arrangements. There is nothing you can do about this—if you don't have the information you can't communicate it.

Let's talk about the family for a moment. Obviously, you have the right to inform your current and former staff and your boss. However, the family may wish to inform the professional and community organizations. Whatever they want is what you do. Ninety-nine percent of the time they are glad to have this burden off their weary shoulders. Often they don't know our profession and won't have the contacts anyway.

Here is one suggestion: you do not have to be the one in contact with the family of your late colleague. There maybe someone else on the staff who is closely connected. Sometimes it is easier for the family to just have one contact within the library and that person then communicates that information to you.

In your communication with the staff, you may wish to state the cause of your late colleague's death. Often, the staff will already know if, for example, your late colleague had a long battle with cancer. However, sometimes the person's mode of dying is not appropriate in your email. For example, you might choose to communicate that it was suicide but now how it occurred. Some staff may be upset that you did not inform them, but you have to remain respectful. You can let staff know privately when they ask, which they will, and word will get out informally. You just don't have to be the one to put it in print. Don't be surprised however to see the mode of passing in a newspaper.

Occasionally, a late colleague may have died under mysterious circumstances and the family does not inform anyone of the mode of passing. Even if you and your staff are very curious, and you all will be, just continue to respect a family's right to be private. I would note that you might actually learn what happened later on as family might tell you when you are expressing your condolences to them or paying your respects to them at the funeral. Again you can let your staff know privately if asked, but again you should not be the one to put it in print.

As often as not, it is one of your staff members who comes to know the reason why your late colleague died and begins sharing that information with others—although often with you first. Most staff will be respectful about sharing the information, but there will be a few who will sensationalize whatever can be sensationalized. You might shake your head at this, but the only action you can take to stop it is to counter with kinder and more respectful words where and when you can.

Understanding how and why a person died is part of the healing process for those who are grieving. While we have to be mindful not to cross the line into morbid curiosity, the fact is that humans are driven at the deepest level to understand mysteries and to uncover the unknown. Not knowing what happened to one of our colleagues leaves something unresolved in our minds like a wound that never completely heals.

Now given a director's busy schedule, you may be away when your colleague passes. You could even be difficult to reach if you are on an international trip. In that case, whoever is the acting director while you are gone needs to send out the message. Then, as soon as you can, you should send out your own personal message. It is much easier to be in constant contact no matter where you are in the world now, but still there are time delays and unreachable moments. Do come back from the trip as soon as you reasonably can. Your staff needs you. Always be there during any crisis within the library.

I want to mention a particular problem in this fast-paced age. If you have a colleague who is passing, you might find that someone has jumped the gun and announced their passing prematurely on social media. This needs to be corrected quickly. It is the result of immature people who want to be the first with information.

ATTENDING THE FUNERAL

I am using the word "funeral" in the generic sense of any service that honors the deceased. There are so many customs, traditions, cultures, religions, and individual and family preferences that can occur.

Whatever it may be, you should attend the funeral, assuming that it isn't private. I also recommend that you go to all of the other arrangements and/or gatherings. If the burial is in a different location from the funeral, go to that. If there is a reception afterward, go to that too. Give time generously to honor the deceased. You certainly don't want to be one of those directors who view the funeral as another task in the day. You are there for your late colleague, there for the family, and there for your staff who are grieving.

Now sometimes directors say that they can't bear to go to funerals as they find the emotional impact too great. Unless you have very good cause, for example, the recent loss of a loved one in your family or other tragedies, be tough with yourself and keep in mind that the funeral isn't about you or your emotions. You are there as a compassionate colleague and as a leader of the library.

You already know that you may have to read up on or ask a knowledgeable staff member about the funeral customs of the religion or culture to which your late colleague belonged. For example, the color and type of flowers that you send on behalf of the library might unintentionally send the wrong message. The color of clothes that you wear, at what time you pay respects to the family, what events to honor the deceased you attend, where you sit in the funeral, and so on are all often dictated by faith and culture.

Back to flowers for a moment. Do send flowers to the funeral on behalf of the library unless the family has specified otherwise. Here you can ask for donations from the staff who truly wish to do something tangible.

Sometimes you will be asked to do a eulogy and naturally you will agree. Make it short and poignant; speak for the whole library while also sharing your personal connection with the person. Also, if you are not doing a eulogy, do be prepared with some words—occasionally, they might throw the microphone open to all and it is good for you to step up and say a few words. One thing I have discovered with listening to eulogies is how little I really knew about a colleague's life even when I thought I knew the person well. The work life is truly just a slice of the totality of a person's life. Unfortunately, funerals are sharp reminders of how much we can be just ships in the night with our colleagues.

Allow all staff who want to go to the funeral to go. Just have minimum staffing that day. Staff also will ask you if you will close the library or the unit where your late colleague worked so all staff can attend. Closing a library or a service is usually only an emergency driven event. Always look for alternatives to closing such as staff from one unit or branch covering for another. Still there are times when it might be appropriate—for example, if you are in a small library where everyone on the staff was close to your late colleague.

Staff will ask you if attending the funeral is on company time. Often company policy is that it is not unless the deceased is a close relative. I suggest that this is one time when you just turn a blind eye to policy.

Now if the funeral is far away, consider giving one or two members of your staff who were close to your late colleague the funds to attend on behalf of the entire library. Soft monies might be able to pay for this.

Now sometimes you will have something scheduled the day of the funeral. Cancel whatever you can. What is harder is the conference trip that is planned, the speech that you are giving, the cruise trip long paid for. What you can cancel, cancel. What you can't, then just go. Focus instead on doing every other tribute that you can in the right way. Now if staff do not see you at the funeral, they will be surprised and puzzled. Therefore, let people know why you cannot attend; otherwise, you will be in for criticism.

PRACTICAL CONCERNS

There is much business to do when a staff member passes away. The life of the library, its services, and the demands of its customers continue regardless. Let's look at the things that need to be taken care of.

First of all, don't be in a hurry. Be respectful—this isn't just another task even if you feel the pressure of work. Let any needed action sit for a while.

Remember these tasks: checking and closing your late colleague's email, posting an email response referring the person to someone else, cancelling appointments, taking care of the mail in the in-box, cleaning out the workstation or office, obtaining the work keys or passes, giving personal belongings back to the family, and removing the name from directories and listservs. Remove the personal computer and have it scrubbed so no personal information remains. However, do keep a backup in a secure location because you might need something that is in there. After about a year, the backup can be eliminated.

Of course, have staff take care of all of these tasks. I have always been impressed how staff rise to the occasion when a colleague passes. They are willing to take on many duties to help with this sad transition. Additionally, they usually think of other things that need to be done. After all, who knows the work of the late colleague better than those who worked side by side?

There are many issues regarding benefits, life insurance, vacation payouts, sick leave, pensions, and so on. Your business manager who handles personnel and financial matters should be in contact with human resources to get started on these issues. Importantly, your business manager should be in contact with the family to help ease the family's way through the bureaucracy.

Sometimes your late colleague had a desirable assignment that another employee always wanted and is bold enough to request this assignment quite quickly afterward. However, make no decisions in a hurry even if you happen to know that a dying colleague wanted this person to have this assignment. Many times, even when facing eternity, employees will be concerned about projects and assignments and make recommendations to you about them. Stop and think about what is best for the library and don't let sentiment rule you. Also, don't criticize the employee who asked for the assignment even if the timing is inappropriate and the actions are opportunistic. This is the way of the world, and people know there is a small window to get what they want.

This brings us to another awkward situation. The business of the library goes on, so you do have to either appoint an interim person or disperse the assignments quickly even if temporarily. If you do it too quickly, you look callous. Do it too late and there can be problems in the work flow, especially if the late colleague held a very pivotal role. There is no magic date on this, but I think it helps if you explain the situation when you inform all staff about the new assignments or the new interim. Your message should show both your reluctance as well as the work necessity. People are realistic and know that the world moves on.

Do leave the person's workstation or office vacant for a while. It is important not to erase all presence of your late colleague quickly. It looks, and is, callous and disrespectful. Frankly no one will want the space for a while anyway, but once again if the office space is desirable you will get early requests for it. Make no decisions on this for quite some time unless there is a compelling work reason.

As soon as possible, do provide counseling services to your staff. Many parent organizations have resident counselors very willing to come in to handle a group meeting or a one-on-one session. If you don't have these resources, get people together yourself—you don't have to try to be an amateur psychologist but you can have an informal gathering to let people speak about their favorite stories or what the person meant to them. Do have a story yourself to start off the conversation.

Continue to walk around and talk with people. Death has a long echo that comes back and back and back to us. People will want to talk about what happened in various ways and at various times. If you are grieving, it is good for you too.

Do cut people slack at this time. Some people won't want to come to work as they do not want to deal with the emotional impact of everyone grieving. Some want to spend longer at lunch and breaks just talking. Some will be walking around talking. Some will stay in their offices and not come out until the end of day. Just let it all flow as staff work out their feelings. And lest you look completely insensitive, only send emails or other messages out to the staff that absolutely must be sent and only require work that absolutely must be done.

Now sometimes your library will have a major event planned right around the time of the passing of your colleague. If you can cancel the event then do so, but often this is not possible. For example, if you have a major public program, a guest speaker, or a media event, then you cannot cancel. Do explain to your staff why you need to continue and again state your regret. If appropriate at the event, do make mention of the passing of your colleague and perhaps have a minute of silence.

A GRATEFUL LIBRARY

Once everyone has been informed about the passing of your colleague, you now must go about honoring your late colleague. I am providing this section for you as a checklist. You undoubtedly know what you need to do but sometimes it is hard to remember everything under the grief of losing a colleague.

If you haven't already done so, do make a formal visit to the family. Take along a colleague with you to help with the conversation because conversation can be difficult at that time. Now sometimes the family lives too far away for you to visit, but at least make a phone call expressing your sorrow and what their loved one meant to the library. A long letter is also appropriate and is something that they can keep and look at in future years.

Here are some of the ways to honor the individual: web pages, a social media page that allows comments and tributes, a plaque in the library, a memory book with cards and photos from the staff for the family, moments of silence, resolutions from the parent organization or elected officials, a video tribute online, scholarships or named awards, and a named donation fund set up to benefit a library service or collection favored by your late colleague.

Sometime after the funeral, do consider a gathering or remembrance to which the family is also invited. The focus should be on a celebration of life. It doesn't have to be very formal—a few speakers, and perhaps a video or photographic tribute. It can be much more of course. Do invite the family to speak but don't be surprised if they can't. Also, the family may ask you if you will do a gathering—and your answer will always be yes. Gatherings are healing for everyone.

Sometimes a tribute will spontaneously occur—for example at your late colleague's work station, in the lobby, on the porch, or wherever. Colleagues and customers may begin to leave objects and notes. If you are asked by your staff if they can set up a tribute, then of course approve it. The difficult piece is when the tribute is in a public area, has religious objects or partisan political items, and you are managing a government-funded library. Usually it is best to be hands off and let people show their grief in the way they want. Fortunately people who might ordinarily object are respectful at this time. Eventually, many of the items and especially the notes can be given to the family.

Now sometimes when everyone is thinking about tributes, some staff may want to name a section of the library after your late colleague. In fact, some may agitate very strongly for this. Unfortunately, this rarely can be done, so you need to address this immediately and frankly. Here is the reason: undoubtedly your parent organization has policies about naming anything and that policy always entails that a large donation has been made. This situation is very awkward but it will come up.

Depending upon the range of activities done to honor your late colleague, many people may have made a contribution of time and effort. Do keep track of who they are and what they did and at the appropriate time send an email thanking everyone for their efforts. They don't expect it, but it is nice to be appreciated.

Do expect honors to go on for about a year or more as people think of things. One question that will come to you is how long should the web pages honoring the person remain. There is no hard and fast rule as you have to gauge the emotions of your staff. I recommend that gradually the web pages are moved from the front page to other sections. If you have a section where former staff are honored, then it can go there and remain there. There is no hurry.

THE YEAR AFTER

Do take steps to remember your late colleague around the first anniversary of passing. Stop by and talk to the staff who were most affected by your late colleague's passing. They will be thinking of the person at this time too and will appreciate that you remembered.

Do enter the date of passing in your next year's calendar because unless you were very close with your late colleague, you won't remember the exact date.

You can also send a letter to the family remembering your late colleague. This letter will have a reflective tone and you will comment again upon the contribution and how much you all miss your colleague.

One problem that does emerge is that after a certain time when a person passes, you begin to hear stories that you really don't want to hear. It can take many forms from behavior in personal life to behavior in the workplace that you knew nothing about. Most of the time, these can be ignored but of course if there was something in the workplace that reverberates into today, then you have to address it discretely. Otherwise, stay silent.

Once in a great while, and long after, a family member, say for example a child who was very young when your colleague passed away, asks you if you or the staff have any memories of their late father or mother. Be sure also to contact retired or former employees to invite them to send memories too.

THE FAMILY OF STAFF

Our focus has been on losing a colleague but I do want to talk about how a director behaves when a staff member loses someone close. First, be careful to make no public announcements until you know your staff member's wishes. Some people prefer complete privacy. Of course, your staff should already know your policy on this—that you respect the wishes of the individual—in case they wonder why you inform them about some tragedies but not about others if they come to learn of them.

If the loss is publicly announced, then certainly invite your staff to send cards and flowers if appropriate. If your colleague has lost a near family member then do go to the funeral.

Don't forget about sending group cards also. Make cards available at a central location, such as library administration, for all your staff to sign. While not everyone will go out and get a sympathy card, almost everyone will stop by and write their sympathies in a group card.

Do make sure that your supervisors and managers report to you immediately when they learn that a tragedy has occurred regarding the family of the staff. I am always surprised at what does not come forward to the director, and it is very awkward to express sympathies when you learn this too late. Do express your sympathies anyway of course.

CONCLUSION

The impact of a death in the library is varied and complex and the ways of grieving are many, so you will do the very best you can but forgive yourself and others if you don't get everything right.

Keep in mind that if there is one word that should capture your actions regarding the death of a colleague: respect. Through every action you take and every word you speak, always have respect in mind. This will carry you through the many issues that you will have to manage when there is a death in the library.

Chapter Nine

Changing Times

No organization can escape the relentless march of change. Is it any wonder that change is a topic widely covered in the management literature? There are literally thousands of books, articles, and research on this complex topic. Well-managed change is one of the keys to a thriving organization. Managers continually seek to understand the management of change in order to succeed.

Your library exists in this ocean of change. Change comes at us from every direction: from the greater environment, from the parent organization, from the profession, from customers, from your staff, and from you. Every library director needs to know how to manage change successfully no matter what its source, because as a director, much of your success hinges on change. You were hired to improve the library's business and delivery systems, to stay up with technology, to modernize customer services, to adapt the building to new needs, to reshape the collection into the digital environment, to create new services, to develop new skill sets in the staff, or to bring in new staff with new talents. The list of things in the change target zone is endless because everything in a library, sooner or later, is in need of change.

But while well-managed change is the way to advance the library's goals, change always comes with its own packet of issues.

No matter how good the change is, no change is trouble-free. In this one chapter, it is not our goal to cover the depth and breadth of the management of change, even if that were possible. Instead I want to focus on the recurring issues of change that every library director should know.

TAKING HEART

It is highly likely that you enjoy change. After all, most of us become directors because we believe that we have the goods to make the library high performing for its customers. A director's position is a creative one as we take the library and mold it in new and exciting ways.

You will be very enthusiastic about a certain proposed change. You see its benefits. You know it will be good for the customers. You don't know why some staff don't see this and why all of the foot dragging is occurring. Why is there anger? Why is there a drop in productivity?

You have just met one of the most frequent problems that come with change: employee resistance. Whenever you start on the path of change, you will meet resistance by some portion of the staff. Sometimes this resistance will be powerful. The resistance may defy logic as the proposed change would be excellent for the library. Otherwise why would you be doing it? However, resistance is not about logic. Change requires effort: new things have to be learned, new steps have to be taken, work stations may change, work groups might be disbanded, job assignments might alter, and so on. Change creates insecurity and, sometimes, fear. You are asking staff to move out of their comfort zone.

Humans are conflicted where change is concerned. On the one hand, we say "a needed change of pace" or "a welcome change." On the other hand, we resist change because it requires us to go to new and uncertain frontiers. The truth is that change is not always beloved.

Here are some ways that staff can resist change: slowing down the work, refusing to learn new tasks, continuing a shadow system of the old process, or giving surface support without any real commitment. Some may act passively by largely ignoring the change in the hope it will go away.

Criticism is also a form of resistance. Even if staff are complying overtly with the change, they might still be providing a steady stream of criticism about the change. If the criticism is useful, then use it, but otherwise just know that it is part of the process. When we ask people to step out of their comfort zones, it increases their anxiety level. Criticism and grumbling are often ways to express and relieve anxiety.

It does seem sometimes that we cannot take a single action without someone commenting critically. Even the simplest things can garner criticism—you might have an event that was a big success with the public but the next day you will hear the criticisms from staff about how it should have been done. Be accustomed to the fact that in libraries we are in endless conversation. Observe it but don't be disheartened by it.

The message here is a simple one: while managing change, don't get disheartened and don't be discouraged from your goals in the face of resistance and criticism. Assuming you have done the due diligence necessary to know that the change is a good one, stay the course. In time, the staff will develop the new skills, adjust to the changes, and reenter their optimum performance zone. When you succumb to resistance and criticism, you have sent a message that you will buckle before you reach your goals. Do this once or twice and you will have trained the staff that resistance to change is acceptable. Moreover, you will have deeply frustrated the staff that supported the change.

PATTERN OF DECISION MAKING

When we think of change in organizations, we often think of the big things—a new service, a new technology system, a renovation, a reorganization, and so on. Such events have a major impact on the life of the library and can radically alter how we do business. However, change also comes about in the daily decisions. As a director, you make a dozen decisions a day. Many of these decisions you make within a short period of time—sometimes just a couple of minutes. Deep analysis isn't done because your experience and savvy works rapidly to inform your choices. In fact, some of these decisions are like breathing in and breathing out because they are so instinctive.

However, each of these decisions—many barely noticeable in the scheme of things—brings micro-change, which adds up over time. Amending a few policies here and there, changing a few procedures here and there, slights shifts in collection development, and so on all contribute to a library that changes gradually over time. The difference is that this change is evolutionary rather than the revolutionary change of big ticket items like a new building.

The important point here is that smaller decisions can over time lead to big changes. Because of this, make sure that your small decisions also have a discernible regularity, a pattern, which continually reflects your priorities and your values. Now, many small decisions are made by your managers and supervisors, so make sure they are on board with making decisions in light of the stated priorities and values. If the pattern of your collective decision making is irregular and not well aligned to your priorities, you could end up with a "crazy quilt"—a haphazard and jury-rigged library.

THE WORLD OF GRAY

Once you take on a director's position, you have left the clear-cut world of black and white behind forever. Because you are now making large-scale decisions around very complex systems involving people, technology, processes, facilities, and so on, you may not always have complete clarity about which way to go. Uncertainty and inexactness now will be regular companions with you in decision making. Add to that your own (and your staff's) parameters, which constrain and cloud decision making: your knowledge, your time limits, and your own abilities.

> ***Ed Evans:*** What every library director should know is ". . . that decision making is never fully risk free. Every decision carries with it some degree of uncertainty and risk no matter how small. The director who has a low risk tolerance runs a long-term chance of being less and less effective. You can increase your risk comfort level, if you wish to do so."

In situations that are ambiguous, you may want to proceed to make a decision anyway. It might be that you do not have and never will have all facts. So you will not have and never will have an optimal solution. But perhaps you have found a workable solution that you and your staff can live with. The question here is always: Does the situation warrant that the solution be optimized or is it good enough? Also keep in mind that decisions in the workplace are rarely forever. Decisions can always be amended or the course corrected.

You can also delay the decision. Just like nature's seasons, decision making also has a winter—a time of hibernation and very little growth. Assuming the building isn't on fire, many decisions can be delayed. If you can't figure out which way to go and nothing seems right, you likely are in the winter of decision making. If you can wait, do so, as the situation may become clearer after a while.

The point here is for you to feel comfortable in the gray world of ambiguity. Ambiguity is now a regular part of your life as a director. All we can do as directors is to make the best decision that we

can even while we acknowledge that we are working in domains in
which the situation is not completely clear.

OUTSIDE FORCES OF CHANGE

We already talked about what happens when a boss wanted change
that was unpalatable to a director. Change, often unpalatable, will
come from other outside forces accompanied by considerable political pressure because of the power of an individual or the power of
a group or agency.

> ***Eleanor Mitchell***: When I started out, I wish I had
> known . . . "the value of opportunity. Well schooled in plan-
> ning and assessment, I have been strategic and intentional in
> setting and pursuing direction in libraries. But in hindsight I
> realize that seizing opportunity, even when it was not foreseen
> or planned, has resulted in the most significant of gains. Even
> the most well-wrought plan should leave open the possibility
> of the unexpected."

Examples of change like this include the following: city councils
that want to merge several departments including the library;
school principals that want to close their libraries to save money
and have the public library pick up the work; a university academic
department that decides to start its own library while expecting
your library to catalog the new collection without any new resources; elected officials that want to develop the property that the
library occupies; building leases that are not renewed leaving the
library without a home; fire departments that want to take the bookmobile for an incident command center; citizen groups lobbying for
a new branch library when there are no resources; citizen groups
resisting the closure of a library that rarely has customers; a friend
of the mayor who makes a large donation with terrible strings at-

tached; or new responsibilities assigned to a director with no raise or new title—under the guise of budget cuts. All of these the author has witnessed and encountered and more.

When you are confronted with proposed change that has political pressure attached, never react quickly in a negative way because you do not want to meet force with force. This will only put people's backs up and put them into fighting mode. Instead, take your time, analyze the situation, think about the agenda behind the proposed change, and consider alternatives.

One problem with reacting quickly and negatively is that you might have lost an opportunity that you would have seen with further analysis, discussion, and reflection. Perhaps the elected officials do want to develop the property the library is on but it could be the start of the library being part of a new and exciting complex of restaurants, theaters, and stores.

Regardless, never buck high-profile people publicly. Do everything behind the scenes. Never be in a public fight. Use charm, graciousness, and humor as much as possible. Also be very careful about using the phrase "it is the principle of the thing." It rarely is, and that is not a statement that you can back down from. Always give yourself an exit strategy.

Sometimes you don't have to react at all. You don't have to respond to everything with a solution or action. Some of this proposed change can just be chatter or just ideas being floated. Be careful though as sometimes these ideas have a life of their own and will keep cropping up, so if it really is a bad idea, you will need to talk with those who are proposing it with a thoughtful response and with equally thoughtful alternatives.

Sometimes when we are confronted with unpleasant and unreasonable change, we also experience anger and frustration. The staff aren't the only ones who experience emotions in response to change. Watch yourself carefully because you don't want your emotions to cloud your judgment. If it does turn out that you have to accept unpalatable change, be careful of your inner resistance and foot dragging: a lot of energy can be spilled resisting change. Resistance distracts the mind, stresses the body, causes a loss of sleep, and increases anxiety—any and all of which can affect your performance as a director, let alone your well-being.

If the change is inevitable, in spite of your best efforts, accept it graciously. The price you will pay is too high if you continue to resist. It could even cost you your job. Just think about how you feel when your staff resist change.

CHANGE FATIGUE

Fatigue is another common issue with change so be mindful of the timing of change. Do be aware that staff can become legitimately worn out by change. If too many changes have come at once, then staff can easily experience change fatigue. Change fatigue is one of the sources of resistance to change.

Watch out particularly if you are a new director. There is a tendency to want to run around and make all the changes that the library needs. After all, you want to get a handle on the library and show that you can do the job. Unfortunately what you have just shown is your inexperience.

Also, how much can you realistically manage yourself? Do you really think that thirty goals is a good idea? Remember that if you push the library hard, you will be pushed back in turn.

The meaning of the word "management" is to control successfully. Too much change shows that you are heedless of the library's total resources. No one can bring that much change to a successful conclusion: failure on many fronts is likely. Take a lesson from botany—how many plants thrive when they have to compete for water and sun and earth? Instead, strive for a balanced workload and achievable goals actually delivered.

Change fatigue can also come through natural disasters such as earthquakes, tornadoes, floods, and fires. Not only is the staff exhausted by trying to get the library back together but also by their home lives, which are usually in the same situation. Any more change at this time is bound to be met with resistance. People are just plain tired.

Be very careful of fatigue when the library staff has been through a lot of budget cuts, which may have even resulted in layoffs or vacancies long unfilled. If you attempt major change at these times beyond what is necessary to accommodate the budget cuts, you will encounter anger, resistance, and distress as well as fatigue. You will also be perceived as someone who is out of touch with the staff.

HANDLING A SETBACK

Change and risk go hand in hand. In our line of work, risk is usually about the potential of an undesirable outcome stemming from any action we have taken. Many people outside libraries assume that there is no risk in our work, but indeed there is. A new OPAC, a reorganization, a capital project, the hiring of personnel, disciplinary actions, a new service or a major change to a current one, and so forth all involve risk.

The course of change never runs smooth. Change is risky business. Sometimes we don't get what we want in planned change: a decision may have gone against us, a grant was not awarded, a project that we thought would be successful turned out to be a less than stellar idea, or an unanticipated problem was buried deep within the change. A library director's life is pockmarked with things that either didn't go our way or didn't quite go the way we thought they would—this is the natural result of going for change.

Sometimes our response to change that was not successful is an angry one. They didn't understand our proposal; the boss decided for his favorites; that person never supports the library; all of her friends voted for her; the vendor is incompetent; human resources messed up; the architect doesn't listen. It may be that these things are true, but instead of shooting from the hip with these comments, do think seriously about what you could have done differently. You and the library must always be in learning mode. Examine closely how you make changes that involve higher degrees of risk with the higher possibility of a setback.

Don't let setbacks reduce your capacity for risk. Sometimes the remembrance of serious setbacks can be a roadblock to future change. Perhaps you really got burned. Keep in mind that getting burned increases our anxiety. Anxiety in turn increases the possibility that we will view future outcomes in a negative or darker light. Our judgment might be clouded by this bad experience. This is particularly an issue for anyone who has less capacity for risk to start with. Fear is the great enemy of change. While getting burned might sting for some time, never let a bad prior outcome get in the way of important future changes.

To add to your frustration about unsuccessful change, there will be a chorus of staff who will claim that they knew that the change would fail all along. They will have no explanation as to why they did not express their concerns at the start—but some staff just prefer to be observers. If the chorus is large though, you may have communication problems. And, of course, all hindsight is 20/20.

Just move on. You have to be able to handle a setback. You can't let setbacks affect you and you can't dwell there either. Certainly you and the affected staff will ponder the setback for a while until the emotions settle down, but don't let yourself or anyone else be a captive of these emotions. Don't let any event be bigger than you.

Often, we have an inkling that something will not go well. I want to stress to you the importance of listening to your intuition. If all your flags are flying, if something doesn't just feel right, if you are bothered by something you can't put your finger on, don't let anyone convince you otherwise or pressure you into change when you don't have that go ahead feeling. Never go against your intuition. It is often said that intuition is reason in a hurry, so somewhere in your mind there is a reason for your intuition. You will handle fewer setbacks if you listen to your management intuition.

Jon E. Cawthorne: What every library director should know is that ". . . becoming a great library leader requires a deep understanding of organizational culture, growth through self-reflection, and a clear, compelling vision; and that each of these improves only through waves of striving and failure."

THE PRICE OF NOT CHANGING

We have all seen libraries that have become stale and listless. The technology is old; no energy or vision remains; the building is out of date; the staff not up with the latest or lazy because little has been asked of them; the librarians restless in their jobs and polishing their resumes; job offers being declined because of the library's poor reputation; the collection off the mark. As time wears on and the problems mount, the library goes into steep decline. It is no longer used and no longer a source of pride.

The price of not changing is very great for any library. A library not engaged in changing is dying slowly as it becomes increasingly irrelevant to its customers. When people don't get what they need from a library, they soon ignore it because now there are so many other information options. The library will also become increasingly irrelevant to its parent organization and even to its own staff.

Whenever you want to think about not changing because the price can be so hard, think about the price of not changing. It takes a while for a library to get into this mess but it comes faster than we think if we neglect change. And, the deeper the library is in this mess, the harder it is to pull it out of the mud.

PROBLEMS WITHOUT SOLUTIONS

Sometimes there will be pressure on us to bring change to solve problems that frankly are without solutions. I want you to give yourself permission to recognize when you have a problem without a solution. This isn't easy because it is the nature of directors to want to solve problems—that is one the vital skills of management after all—so we don't admit defeat easily.

Building issues are classic examples of problems without solutions. Some buildings just no longer meet current needs and could desperately do with a change, but there is little to no chance of a major renovation or a new building. Another example is inadequate parking—this annoying situation to customers and staff alike is often something that just has to be lived with.

Sometimes the staff will nag at us to solve problems that you know are without solution. It is okay to listen once or twice, but after that close off the conversation. Explain that you understand the problem but there is not currently a solution so let's go on to change that is possible. Otherwise, this problem will be on every agenda.

James L. Mullins: "Since I am nearing the end of my career as a librarian/library administrator after nearly forty years, I feel privileged to have witnessed the change in academic libraries firsthand. When I started as a cataloger in 1973, we ordered cards from the Library of Congress, typed on title and subject headings, filed the cards in the catalog that replaced temporary slips that had been filed two to three years earlier. Today the bibliographic record is in the online catalog as the item goes on the shelf or, more and more often, has been acquired as a digital copy and available to a user anywhere he or she might be.

"Looking back nearly forty years allows me to see the progression of changes, sometimes steady and sometimes through a disruptive change such as the implementation of OCLC or CD towers for database access. However, once the bugs were worked out, the benefits to the user and staff were apparent. Even if it were possible to return to the 'old days,' none of us would do it.

"Today when I experience resistance to a change in the library, that to me seems more or less 'fine tuning' something that started nearly forty years ago, I try to remember the stressful times caused by a change in the past and empathize. After each of those past disruptive changes, it wasn't long before it was recognized that the change was always for the better."

PROJECT MANAGEMENT

Here is one tip that will help you to manage change successfully. Take training in the field of project management. Project management is about planning, controlling, and motivating the resources of any organization toward achievable goals. The philosophy, strategies, and skills of project management are applicable to any field of change. Project management identifies a sequence of steps from the conceptualization of the change all the way to completion. Following this sequence in the management of change helps us to avoid many of the pitfalls and problems of change. Importantly, project management helps us to manage the three continual constraints of change: time, cost, and scope. Project management is an excellent skill for you and key staff to have.

CONCLUSION

You can never read too much about change. It is a vital skill for every library director. As you approach change, just always have the above points in mind in order to minimize the many challenges that come with change.

For further writings by me on change, see Managing Change, Revised Edition, New York: Neal-Schuman, 2005.

Chapter Ten

Transitions

Two of the most challenging periods in any director's life are starting and ending a job. Both of these important transitions require
skillful management for the sake of the library and for the director.
We are going to look now at what every library director should
know about starting the job and finishing the job whether as a result
of being fired, resigning, or retiring.

STARTING THE NEW JOB

You can never to be too careful when you are starting a new job.
Most of the time how well you manage your first year will determine how your staff, your supporters, your boss, or your colleagues
in the parent organization will think of you. If you goof, you will be
repairing your image for a long time. If you commence successfully, you will enjoy everyone's collective sense of your competence.
Their good opinion of you will create a firm foundation for your
tenure. You will be acknowledged as the right person for the job.

Remember that your job as a director starts the day that you
accept the job and not the first day that you are paid. You cannot
wait until you are actually on the job. There are things that you
want to do in those first weeks on the job that must be set up now.

For example, there may be meetings that you will want to hold on your first day on the job. You cannot wait until you are there to have meetings set up, otherwise you will lose precious time.

Another reason you will begin working ahead of your start date is because staff and the outgoing director may need to consult with you about upcoming decisions and actions that will occur right as you start the job. Just remember that you don't know the environment or the politics so take your time in decision making. Make sure it is something that you really need to decide now.

> *Virginia Walter:* When I started out, I wish I had known . . . "the importance of listening."

Talk to the current director about what you will need during this transition period including meeting with key staff to get up to speed on various projects. On the one hand, you want to be respectful by not treading on the territory of the current director; on the other hand, you have to start your job. Most outgoing directors will do what they can to help with this transition.

Commence with a good relationship with the director's secretary. This person is pivotal in your life, and the stronger the relationship, the better. With the current director's knowledge, take the secretary to lunch, get to know each other and talk about the ways of working together. Getting a new boss is a very nervous time for a secretary, so the more you ease that nervousness, the more successful you both will be. If you are asking the secretary to set up meetings for you, or send you reports and other information, be mindful of the secretary's workload for the current director. Overloading the secretary isn't a good start to the relationship.

In the early days, make no commitment to the secretary's job security. You have to take time to get to know the person so don't trap yourself by making any commitments in case it turns out that you are not suited for each other. Don't be surprised though if the secretary starts looking for a new job. Don't take it personally because often it is just a good opportunity for the secretary who might be ready to move on. Most secretaries also realize that the new boss wants to have his or her own person. In fact, it will be an opportunity for you if you come to the reality that the current secretary will not meet your expectations. A secretary who moves on by his or her own volition solves the problem of you looking like the bad guy.

In order for a secretary to be effective support to you, it is important that he or she be kept in the loop for all matters pertaining to your job—including confidential matters. However, you should gradually test your secretary's ability to be confidential. You are after all strangers, and your secretary has as yet developed no loyalty to you. Don't risk too much confidential information too soon but just now and then. If you don't spot any leaks, you can risk a bit more. The problem is that it can take a while to discover that your secretary is leaking information, but eventually it all gets back to you. If you find out that your secretary is not confidential, then he or she has to be removed. You can't risk leaks from your office.

If it turns out that you have inherited an excellent secretary who wants to stay, rejoice! Your life as a director will be much easier with the solid support that only a good secretary can give.

As you transition, dig deep into the library's history by reading annual reports, web pages, budgets, personnel charts, planning documents, union contracts, and so forth. Much of this you will have done before you interviewed, but now the information will take on a new urgency. The purpose of extensive reading is to be partially up to speed so that you have a background on and a framework for issues. From your readings, you will also develop a set of questions about library services and projects that need clarification.

While you are at it, be sure to read all of the rules, regulations, charters, and laws relating to your library. It is a good idea to master the legal environment of your library early so you are always walking the straight and narrow and always aware when you might be steering close to a violation. (While you are thinking about legal matters, take a moment and learn how subpoenas are handled too. It is not uncommon in the life of a library to receive a subpoena for customer records or sequestered archives.)

Be wary of staff that are very quick to want your ear. Listen, but form no opinions, make no promises, and forge no alliances. Be very mindful of your actions because they could have far-reaching consequences. You will of course at this time be barraged by welcome emails and the like. Most of that is genuine and part of it is survival as the staff want to get on the right side of the new boss. After all, an important power shift has just occurred. Just respond graciously and make no commitments because often you may find a request or a statement concerning an issue embedded in that email.

Everyone talks about a honeymoon period as you start a new position. To some extent that is true as people sincerely want you to succeed and genuinely wish you well. Be aware though of the undercurrents of the politics which are always in play.

For example, you might experience either overt or covert hostility if there was another favored candidate who works in the library already, or worse, may be the interim director. There might be camps that supported you or the other candidate. While you don't have to put up with nonsense such as surly behavior or inadequate responses to your requests for information or malicious gossip from the other camp, just keep moving forward and doing your job the best you know how. Eventually, everyone accepts the reality and does come round. Don't expect them to be your boosters though, not now and possibly not ever.

One challenge that can occur is when you learn that the internal candidate is politically well connected. We discussed in chapter 3 about what to do with politically connected staff. However, don't trouble yourself too much in thinking about the internal candidate's connections. After all, how powerful were those connections if their buddy, the internal candidate, did not get the job?

If there was an internal candidate who also was the interim director, make every effort to treat this person with respect. Make sure that he or she is publicly thanked. However, if there is persistent hostility toward you from the interim, have a frank conversation with him or her about this behavior because you cannot be disrespected in the job by anyone. Hopefully, he or she will see the error of their ways and will not want to pay the price of continued hostility toward you: behavior that can result in dismissal.

Now usually an interim returns to the position that he or she had before being interim director. Sometimes there is no maneuverability on that, but if there is, consider two things. First, it is your decision what position the interim will now hold. Don't be on automatic. Second, think about putting the interim into another interim position until you are sure you that you have this person's support and you know his or her true capabilities and interests. That will also give you more flexibility if you want to do a reorganization sooner rather than later.

Speaking of reorganizations, this is the favorite activity of all new directors. Unless the library is in total disarray and immediate and dramatic action is called for, the watchword for reorganizations is "easy does it." Reorganizations done poorly can be a simmering source of resentment for a long time. Study the work flow, consult with your staff, understand the reasoning for the existing organizational structure, work with human resources, keep everyone in the loop, and then roll out the reorganization in a controlled manner. Even then staff will need training and resources if there are substantial changes to their jobs. Don't be in a hurry to reorganize. Take your time; do it right.

Give priority to your staff. Get to know them, their names, their jobs, and a bit about their family or background. It is always tempting to dive right into plans and goals, but remember plans and goals are only successful when people help you to carry them out. Your new staff has to begin to bond with you, and the only way to achieve that is to spend time with them. With good luck and good management, you may work together for a long time, so create the relationships now that you wish to have in the future.

Sometimes your predecessor has not come to a good end on the job. Sometimes the interim was seriously underskilled for the position. This means that there is a power vacuum because any weakness at the top results in parts of the job not being done or being done badly. Staff may have taken control of the various parts of the director's job either because they were trying to do what needed to be done or because they were seeking power. Regardless, take up the reins of power quickly. Do the director's job and don't be influenced by who is doing what now. For the staff that were altruistic and doing the work for the good of the whole, keep them in mind for future jobs. For power-grabbing staff, don't let them head you off at the pass by false reasons as to why they should keep on doing what they were doing.

More often than not, you will begin to hear stories about your predecessor, and sometimes they are not good ones. It might be about how the budget was handled, or personnel matters that went bad or issues that weren't dealt with. Worse, it might be about personal behaviors, relationships, or alcoholic tendencies. It is important to watch your own responses to this gossip. On the one hand, you want to listen to good staff that could be providing background or context, advising you where the minefields are or giving you a heads-up. On the other hand, you don't want to develop a reputation as a director who likes to gossip and get the goods on people. Just listen briefly—you can't escape it—and you might hear important information. Just never indulge and ask "then what?" in a fascinated tone to juicy gossip. Always maintain an attitude of respect for your predecessor as you wish yourself to one day be respected when you are gone from the job.

When a new director comes in, a lot of gossip surrounds the individual. There are the people who want to be known to be in the know and who are sharing with others all they know about you—often inaccurately. There are people who like to make predictions about how long you are going to stay. There are people who are clear on what your priorities and agendas are. While you have to be mindful about gossip, and counter anything that is dangerous to your reputation or too silly, just be aware that people talk about the boss. Again, just move forward and do your job—what you want is for people to talk about your competence and capability.

This next point is for those of you who are brand new directors. As one of the most visible faces of the library, you do have to look the part. Remember that dressing, like all art, sends a message. You don't have to appear in expensive power suits every day but look and see what your peers, your boss, and your boss's boss are wearing. Then steadily and surely take on the symbols of the position by dressing appropriately for your library and your environment.

I know that some of you may say that the issue of dressing the part is superficial. No, it isn't. Staff want to be proud of you. They want a director that every other library envies. They want to hear you praised and to know that they have the best. They want to know that you are popular and well liked. They enjoy that you are considered highly effective in your role. You are doing a good job and it shows. It gives your staff pride.

Your personal image, the look, is part of this success. Never forget that you are always in the business of image making. Now, for you free spirits, I am not suggesting that you be someone that you are not and that you take on a persona that isn't yours just because everyone else is like that—but there is a balance between being completely co-opted by the culture of an environment and being indifferent to it.

Start out on the job being mindful of the condition of your office. Honestly, a messy, cluttered office is not charmingly eccentric nor does it send the message that you are busy beyond belief. The message is sends it that you are messy, disorganized, and have no control over the work flow. Start out right with your office and keep it right. Your office should transmit a message of calm serenity and control.

Now what happens if you make a major goof when you are first starting out? This can take any form and can be from any number of reasons: inexperience, misreading of the situation, assumptions based erroneously on past experiences, or trusting those who should not have been trusted, and so on. You have goofed and the staff, and possibly your boss, is mad and disappointed. You might be horrified and not want to come to work that day or even that week, but soldier on. Apologize, correct the mistake immediately, and then stop dwelling on it. And don't keep apologizing. Sometimes we want to keep apologizing because we are very anxious about the situation. But your anxiety must not be played out in the organization. Yes, your goof will be talked about for some time and it will be embarrassing, but you have to be able to handle a setback. How you manage your goof is important, and it will go a long way to reclaiming your reputation.

PROMOTED FROM WITHIN

Now what if you were already working in the library before you were appointed the director? Usually this works out well because you already know the library's history, goals, projects, issues, and people. You have friends and allies. While all of this powerful knowledge and those connections will work to your advantage, you want to be careful about your existing opinions about issues and people. Watch and examine your prejudices and preconceived notions carefully. From the perspective of your new responsibility for the entire library, look at projects, goals, and issues afresh. From your new angle, look at people afresh. Now, some of your opinions may change naturally because you will have access to information that you did not have before. In time, it will dawn on you that as a result of self-awareness, new knowledge, and a new perspective, a number of things will look different.

We discussed in chapter 3 how your relationships with your friends in the library may now change. Even though your days will be busy, busier than you may ever have been, do keep up with your friends. There is no link like old links to people, and the best of your friends will still be there for you during this transition time and will provide tangible and intangible support.

Sometimes you will have competed against a friend or ally for the director's job. In this situation, both parties during the interview process are usually gracious and overtly wish the other person success. There is an element of survival in this graciousness. No one wants to make an enemy of someone who could soon be the director. Once you are selected, your rival will experience some jealousy, possibly hostility, and may also feel humiliated. Most mature people get over this fast realizing that this is the competitive process. Give your rival time to settle back in. Treat your rival normally. When your rival congratulates you, as usually occurs, just respond graciously. Any demonstrated compassion at this time will only be patronizing.

ACCIDENTAL DIRECTOR

Sometimes you find yourself in an interim director position even though it has never been your career goal. Perhaps no suitable candidates are coming forward for the permanent position. Perhaps the current director left the position suddenly leaving the library in the lurch. There you are: the most likely person to run the library. Just do the job as if you were the permanent director. An interim director who has a caretaker attitude can do a lot of damage because the library will begin to run down if there is no energy at the top. This doesn't mean that you decide to take on a new capital project or do a reorganization, but move forward with the goals that are on the table. Now you might face resistance from some staff who will regard you as a short-timer who should not be moving goals forward. After all, isn't the new director going to change everything anyway? Maybe, but explain that the library can't just be spinning its wheels until the permanent director arrives—which sometimes can be a year or more. Good staff will support you in moving the library forward because they don't want the library to run down either. Even one year of no action can set a library back.

By the way, unless you are 100 percent sure that you do not want the permanent director's job, don't publicly or privately comment that you have no intent or interest in applying for the position. You might find when you are in the position for a while that you do like it and have the talent for it. Your staff might be urging you to go for it. So leave the option of applying open in case you decide you want to throw your hat in the ring.

JOB SHOCK

A job often looks very different from the inside than from the outside. You may have wanted this position your entire career but do be prepared that you will have some moments of fear and doubt about your readiness for the job. Any anxiety is natural especially since you have just put yourself in major change and stepped up to responsibilities that you did not have before.

Keep in mind that you are in a learning curve. Whether you are a new director or new to the position, you will be in an ocean of learning when you take on a new job. It is said that 80 percent of learning occurs the first year on the job. It is a steep climb. Do cut yourself some slack. By the way, although rest and relaxation will be the furthest thing from your mind, rest and relaxation, wherever and whenever you can get it, is vital to keep up your energy and alertness.

Now you might have inherited a disastrous situation. The budget is in disarray, the staff are fighting, bad hires have been done, the buildings are a mess, the customers are up in arms, the collections are out of touch, and the service is poor. The culture of the library is toxic with fear, and caution rules the actions of the staff. The staff have long ago abandoned their imagination and drive. The librarians are dusting off their resumes. Your new boss might have told you during the interview that the library needed some better management, but the true scale of it might make you want to close your office door and put your head in your arms. You might be asking yourself "Is this what I signed on for?" or "What on earth have I done?" Just remember this is why you were hired after all. Prioritize the problems, roll up your sleeves, and get started.

Phil Turner: What every library director should know . . .
"is to never make a decision when you are angry."

However, in a situation like this, as you begin to solve problems, never think that you are at the bottom of the barrel of problems. When a library has been badly managed over a long period of time, the waters are very deep. It is very likely that for years you will encounter problems you had no idea existed.

If you are new to being a director, one thing that helps is to build up a network of fellow directors. While you will naturally be careful about anything confidential, there is much that can be discussed. As a new director, you will be amazed at how much libraries have in common, and hearing fellow directors with the same problems and issues is very comforting.

THE END OF THE LINE: FIRED

Getting fired is a drastic and often heartbreaking experience. It could occur for any number of reasons. Perhaps there has been a serious financial, legal, or mismanagement problem in your library. Perhaps you were caught in the buzz saw of city politics. Perhaps you have a new boss who wants to be surrounded with his or her own people or who wants to be a new broom. Perhaps your library was swept up in a controversy and you have become the focus of the perceived problem. Or perhaps the library is being merged with another department and a director at your level is no longer needed. The list goes on.

Your emotions will be very powerful when you are being fired—all the more so if the firing is very sudden and without warning. These emotions are a strong stew of shock, horror, anger, and embarrassment. There is a sense of the unfairness of it all. Very quickly comes worry, especially if you are the main support of a family or even just like to support yourself. We all know how quickly we can go from being successful to struggling to find work. Fear is a natural response.

If you have an inkling that you likely will be fired, pull out your contract, which should have an agreed-upon exit package, and refresh your mind as to the terms. Need I remind you of the importance of having a contract with an exit package? Having an exit strategy is vital because most directors serve at the pleasure of the board, the president or chief executive officer, or the city manager, which means gone in sixty minutes.

Now if you didn't get an agreed upon exit package at hiring—and not every organization does that—start thinking about what you want as you exit. Regardless of your preparation though, if you are offered a package as you are being dismissed, don't agree to it on the spot. If you can, get some time to think it over. Remember that in the moment of being fired, your emotions will cloud your usual clear thinking and judgment. Any reaction at this time is not optimal.

There may be other documents that you will be asked to sign when you are being dismissed. Consider the consequences of any such documents. For example, if you are asked to sign that you are resigning willingly, you likely have negated the possibility of early retirement or unemployment benefits. Again, try to buy some time to think about what they are asking you to sign. And also why: no mystery there—it is because they are protecting themselves and/or the parent organization. Only you will be able to protect you.

Speaking of resignations, you may wish to consider resigning before you are fired if you have gotten yourself into some hot water. This preemptive action sometimes calms things down as your boss and human resources will view this as a nonconfrontational, easier way out. From their perspective, problem solved! Yes, there are consequences to resigning as we just discussed, but it might be preferable to getting fired if it is for cause. Remember also that the firing of a director eventually becomes public knowledge and, in the case of public or academic directors, is usually in the press. Having a narrow escape by resigning might be better than having your reputation damaged in the press. While your resignation might be news and while there will be gossip, still this is better than the headlines of being fired.

If financial or legal problems are brewing on a scale that could lead to dismissal or worse, whether you are in the wrong or not, get an attorney.

Now sometimes a director has been accused unjustly and dismissed unfairly. If you get caught up in this terrible situation, then take every action needed to protect your reputation including speaking to the press. You are going down for the count anyway— why should your accusers have the last word? And of course, you will have an attorney to protect your rights and benefits and guide you through the morass.

Now if you are the director/dean of a university library where
your librarians have faculty status, you usually have retreat rights to
a faculty position. If you are able and willing to exercise this option, ask for paid administrative leave for at least a few weeks or
possibly even a semester so that there is time between your dismissal from the job and starting work as a librarian. Often you will get
some administrative leave to "re-tool" because your boss, human
resources, and possibly even your staff don't want to see you the
day after dismissal either. When you start work again, hold your
head up high, be the best librarian that you can be, and become a
real member of the team. And never comment on what the interim
director or your eventual successor is doing.

If you still wish to be a director regardless of how you are
exiting your director position, get back into the job market as soon
as you can. It won't be easy. If you have been fired or have resigned suddenly, you have a lot of baggage to overcome no matter
what the reasons. However, get going, because otherwise you add
to the problem by having a long gap in employment which is also
tough to explain on a resume.

Consider activating your network to see if your fellow directors
know of any opportunities that are coming up but not yet public.
Now if you don't want to connect with fellow directors because the
cause for your firing is something you were hoping to keep a lid on,
don't worry about it. Your fellow directors, especially those in
geographic proximity, likely will have heard all about it from their
staff who has heard all about it from your staff.

Of course, as a general practice, it is a good idea to always read
the job ads even when you are not looking so you are constantly
aware of what is available. And of course, always have your resume up to date.

If you do think it likely that you will be fired, do begin very
discretely to take home personal items. Do it unobserved because
you want to avoid signaling to your staff that you suspect you will

be fired. Remember that it is possible that you may have to clear out of your office the day that you are dismissed or you might even be walked off the premises. Therefore, you want to have as few possessions as possible in order for you to pack quickly or, in really bad situations, for someone else from the parent organization to pack for you.

Do back up your computer so you can take the back-up home. You never know what you might need. Delete or otherwise clear up your files, searches, and emails on your office computer. If you were given a mobile phone or tablet, back that up too especially your contacts which you may need. Remember you will be cut off from access to all technology once you are gone. Also, shred or discard paper files very discretely. If you are being fired for anything illegal, don't delete or shred even if it is innocuous. Remember: obstruction of justice is a serious matter—don't compound the problem you are already in. Of course, they probably have seized all of the relevant files anyway.

If you were fired for just cause, you might not have time to say goodbye to your colleagues. Try to reach key people but be aware that if the circumstances are bad, they actually won't want to hear from you for fear that they might be implicated in some way. They may also be very angry that you got yourself and the library into a mess.

Now you might say to yourself, what if I had an inkling, took these actions, and the firing did not come to pass? Then just consider yourself lucky and admire your newly uncluttered office. If you got yourself into trouble, then make darn sure that nothing you do in the future gets you into that situation again. Deeply evaluate what happened and what caused you to get yourself into such a pickle. You might want to think about looking for a new job anyway because your brand has been tarnished if you were that close to disaster.

While you are employed, do think about having another string to your bow because of the reality of our hiring contracts. Don't just be a one trick pony but always be aware of other options and even other careers. This isn't easy when you have focused all your efforts and time on being a good director, but these are uncertain times and you may want to see if you can develop some expertise in another area.

THE END OF THE LINE: RETIRED

With a bit of luck and careful planning, the end of the line is retiring. Hopefully you will be leaving a well-staffed, financially fit, and beloved library. Your legacy is secure.

As you approach retirement, create a checklist of things to do. You won't have a do-over so you need to get it right. Think about tasks that must be done. Think about people you need to thank. Think about people, such as donors, that you need to see for farewells. Keep adding to the checklist. Ask your immediate staff if there is anything they need particularly before you go. They will appreciate it because there may not be another time like this to make certain requests.

Be generous to your successor. Arrange to have your office painted after you leave but before your successor comes. Leave soft monies so your successor has some funds for projects right away. Leave some positions vacant so your successor has room to maneuver in a reorganization. Leave important reports in an otherwise completely cleared out office. If your successor wishes, go to lunch and answer any questions that he or she may have. After all, you do want your successor to be successful.

Be wary of being considered a short-timer. Yes, you will get jokes and you will get tired of those jokes—most of the time it is just affectionate. However, your work habits should not change. Stay on top of the job until the last minute. A person with a short-timer attitude is a problem in the workplace, and a director with a short-timer attitude can do a lot of damage by being inattentive to the work.

So, enjoy your last weeks or months with the library and with your career, but don't relax too much. The vigilance which you used throughout your career is the same vigilance you use now. Remain attentive to what is going on because you can still have a disaster even on your last week. You don't want to end on a low note.

Sometimes when we get near the end, we really begin to lose patience. The meeting which seems to have the same agenda, the staff member who endlessly complains about the same unresolvable issue, the nonsense behavior can really get to us. While you might not be able to take that meeting one more time, remember you are still getting paid and you still have a job to do. Curb your tongue and think of your legacy—this is not a time to tell people how you really feel about this or that. They will remember a last bad year more than any other thing.

Also, when retired, curb any inclination to gossip about your successor with your former colleagues. Never forget that your comments could be repeated to your successor—and that is not a situation that you want. It is particularly hard not to gossip if it turns out that your successor isn't quite up to it. Instead, give your successor space and time—your successor has a big job now especially if he or she hasn't been a director before.

It is also hard not to gossip when your successor seems to be systematically undoing every important project or decision that you made. Remember that you made your decisions in a certain time and your successor is doing the same thing. After all, didn't you do the same thing to your predecessor? Just let your ego go and get on with your new life.

James L. Mullins: "Finally, one bit of wisdom that has come with experience (and advancing age) is that we follow a long line of dedicated professionals who worked within the parameters of their time. Those of us who have had the responsibility and opportunity to guide the course of academic libraries built upon the environment we inherited; just as those who will follow will build upon the environment they are bequeathed. It is not important what an individual administrator accomplishes; it is the cumulative work of those who have come before, those at present, and those who will come. As a library administrator, whether dean, director, or university librarian, we are stewards for a brief period of time in the history of the academic research library, and to quote Robert Baden-Powell, 'Always leave a place better than you found it.'"

THE END OF THE LINE: RESIGNED

Here, I want to focus on resigning from a director's position to take a new director's position. It can be quite tricky. The problems come during the job search. The librarian profession is highly networked and highly social, so word will always get out. Additionally, many finalists become public knowledge because the interviews are often public—this is especially true in a university or public setting. Never think that no one will know that you are interviewing. I suggest that you share this information right before it becomes public to key staff. That way, they won't be caught by surprise and can also field questions from other staff.

People will ask you why you want to leave. A common comment is "I thought you were happy here." Your answer is that you are and if the new job doesn't turn out then you will be very happy to remain. This is just an opportunity for you. Never say it will be good for the library too because it is time for change—that will give people ideas.

Be careful about other words and actions while you are interviewing for the other job. Don't start cleaning out your office. Don't send out messages about how much you have enjoyed working there. Don't start coming in late or making jokes about "I'm outta here." You really don't know the outcome, and if you fail to succeed, then you will have done yourself some serious damage by transmitting a complete lack of commitment to the library.

Of course, you will need to let your boss know that you are interviewing before the interview becomes public knowledge. It won't go well if the boss hears from someone else, which in the chatting world of libraries certainly will occur. Do be very prepared for this conversation. After all, if you don't get the job, you still want the one you have. Watch your boss's face very carefully. If the boss is genuinely upset, then you know you are okay. If the boss is matter of fact or seems indifferent, then you might want to keep on the job market.

If you do accept the new position, be prepared to encounter some negative or unhappy emotions from your library colleagues—this could range from jealousy that you are going to a desirable job to anger that you are abandoning the ship to fear as to who will succeed you to genuine sadness that you are going. You should expect that most will be happy for you—and this will be true—but don't get caught by surprise at the complexity of emotions around your leaving. It will not be complete joy for you either as there is always the sadness of parting.

Now it gets even trickier when you don't get the job and have to settle back into your current position. Just get back to work. It is surprising how soon much of this is forgotten. People are realistic and they are also not sitting around speculating about your life all the time.

As a footnote, never leave a director's job because you are angry or frustrated. Those genuine emotions might propel you to look for a new position, but the actual decision to move must be based on a cool calculation. You should never decide to leave your job based on "I'm done with this place!" Instead, decide if this move is the next logical step in your career. Will this move benefit you and/or your family in tangible or intangible ways? Will this new position fulfill your heart's desire? We only have this one life—shape it carefully.

TRAVELING LIGHT

As a footnote, I want to talk about the importance of always "traveling light" in your job. A director's job is a precarious one and you never know when the transition will come. While you want to be and should be confident and comfortable in your job, never get to feeling at home. Keep very few personal items in your office—you should be able to pack up with only a couple of boxes. Make sure that you are on an annual cycle of shredding or discarding files and papers, sending some files to the administrative archives and cleaning up your office computer. Never have anything personal on any office technology. I know this seems harsh, but some directors really burrow into their offices and it takes days, which they might not have, to clear out. Never forget that you only inhabit that office for such and such a period of time and that the ending of that time is not always known to you.

CONCLUSION

During any major transition, the watchword is mindfulness. Be attentive inwardly and outwardly. Stay centered. Listen actively. Manage with all of your skill and ability. This way, you will start the job successfully and with bit of luck, end the job at a time of your choosing. Keep looking forward and moving forward—a new chapter in your life is opening.

For further writings by me on this subject, see "Retiring Graciously" in a book entitled *Pre- and Post-retirement Tips for Librarians*, edited by Carol Smallwood, Chicago: American Library Association, 2012.

A Final Word

I had the opportunity to manage special, public, and academic libraries in the course of my career. As I mentioned in the introduction, what I wrote about in this book is the knowledge that I gained from extensive experiences that either I had, or observed or that were shared with me by fellow directors, colleagues, bosses, faculty, library supporters and customers, and board members. As you have seen throughout this book, this knowledge is not exclusive to any one type of library. The practices, principles, and experiences in this book are relevant to all libraries.

I have now concluded my career, but I wanted to pass on to the current and coming generations of library directors what I learned throughout my long career. I may not have covered everything in this book, but I hope that I covered most of the important topics and issues that every library director should know in order to be successful on the job.

Good luck in your career as a director. Be sure to pass on to the next generation what you have learned!

Susan Carol Curzon

Index

About the Author

Dr. Susan Carol Curzon is Dean Emeritus of the University Library of California State University, Northridge. Previous positions include director of libraries for the City of Glendale, California, and regional administrator for the County of Los Angeles Public Library. She also has experience in a corporate library. Her doctorate is in public administration from the University of Southern California and her M.Libr. is from the University of Washington. She was *Library Journal*'s "Librarian of the Year" in 1993. Library management, disaster management, and information literacy have been the primary topics of her numerous speeches and articles. She is the author of *Managing the Interview* (1995) and *Managing Change* (2005) and the coeditor and commentator of *Proven Strategies for Building an Information Literacy Program* (2007, with Lynn D. Lampert). Dr. Curzon continues to provide consulting services for libraries, for universities, and for municipalities on strategic management, disaster recovery, and building planning. She lives in Los Angeles and Honolulu.

Dr. Curzon can be contacted at susan.curzon@csun.edu.

CPSIA information can be obtained at www.ICGtesting.com
Printed in the USA
BVOW04s2021010414

349428BV00002B/3/P